MW01502550

Love, Laughter
& Losing My Keys

To Johanna,

   Best wishes for loads of love and laughter despite having to live with Santa.

   Love from me —
   Emily Braddock Jones
   2014

Love, Laughter
&
Losing My Keys

(A Boomer's Guide to Survival)

Emily Braddock Jones

CROOKED CREEK PROPERTIES

Library of Congress Control Number
2014912109

Printed in the United States of America

Cover design by Joe Lee and Cyndi Clark
Cover photo and author photo by Leilani Salter (www.leilanisalter.com)
Chapter opening artwork of the four seasons by Nel Slaughter
The Fifth Season photograph by Caroline Harrell Atkins

Other photographs © iStock: Clothespins: onairjiw | Coffee: Chris_Elwell
Dustcloth: abramovtv | Facial tissue: EuToch | Garden tools: gualbertobecerra
Glasses: nandoviciano | Keys: lotax | Lollipops: loooby | Makeup: Elenathewise
Notepaper: sak12344 | Ornaments: Boltenkoff | Pizza: caimacanul | Popcorn: joebelanger
Purse: agentry | Sticky note: lior2 | Takeout: rimglow | Wand: SDenson

First edition October 2014

CROOKED CREEK PROPERTIES
www.deludeddiva.com
crookedcreek47@gmail.com

To my father, Dr. Tom Braddock, and my stepmother, Martha Braddock, who teach me every day that laughter is still the best medicine. And to my sons, Braddock and William, who taught me how to use the computer so I could write this book.

In loving memory of my mother, Vivian.
I close my eyes and I can still see her smile.

Contents

Contents

Acknowledgments

When we decided to put our adventures and special recipes into a book, we brought in the only person on the planet who could understand our story. Nel Slaughter, an award-winning artist, teacher, and close friend, agreed to help us put the whole project together and give it some style and color. She believed in what we were doing and brought some sanity to our little ragtag editorial team. Thank you, Nel, for the beautiful artwork celebrating the seasons of life.

I am beyond grateful to my editor, Joe Lee, who took the project and gave it new life when it was but a ghost of an idea.

Thanks also to my friend and fellow Mississippi author Laurie Parker for creative and technical support. And thanks to my oldest son, Braddock, who reassured me and reminded me that "it ain't Moby Dick" when it came to the subject matter of my book.

And last, but certainly not least, my heartfelt thanks goes to Nita Keys Wyman of West Point. She was only a few years older than the Class of '65 when she became our high school English teacher. Not only was she my favorite high school teacher, she has become a good friend who agreed to eyeball this rambling manuscript for grammatical errors. I suspect she agreed to the chore to avoid embarrassment should it be published in its original form and reveal that I didn't listen very carefully in her classes. It was full of typos, which for the life of me I cannot spot, along with numerous dangling participles and a conspicuous lack of commas. I write like I speak—nary a comma lest someone get a word in edgewise.

Emily Braddock Jones

9

Introduction

My friend Margaret Ann Wood and I acquired one of life's most prized possessions in the last will and testament of our dear friend Linda Murrah Clark, who died in 1999 after a valiant battle with ovarian cancer.

She left us the most precious of gifts—our friendship. Up until her death we competed to be her best friend. But she knew her time was short and suspected we could only fill the void caused by her death by sealing our friendship with each other. We became irreversibly and deeply bonded on the long drives from our hometown to the Mississippi Delta, where Linda spent the last nine years of her life (married to a dashing Delta farmer). Though she was gravely ill, she always seemed to enjoy our company and more specifically—Margaret Ann's cooking.

During those jaunts back and forth, we would talk nonstop about life, love, food, and dieting—usually in the reverse order. Before her death Linda commented that it would have been a treat to be a fly on the dashboard during those trips. It wouldn't have been very productive because we have the habit of talking (loudly) at the same time and jumping from topic to topic until we are exhausted and "talked out."

Having lost our mothers at an early age, Margaret Ann and I were touched to the core when Linda asked us to look after her mother, Mrs. Martha Ganss of West Point, Mississippi. We kept our promise—not just for Linda but also because "Mama M" endeared herself to us as only the best mamas do.

Mama M is with Linda now, and they are cookin' away up there with the saints. Till we meet again . . .

. . .

We've added a fifth season, which Baby Boomers know all too well. We call it "Baby Boomers Busting Loose," because to our surprise growing older has turned out to be a glorious time of life (which we could never have anticipated when we were young, and life stretched before us as far as we could see). The great thing about "booming" is that with children grown and careers winding down, we finally have time to pursue our dreams . . . which are taking surprising and fearless twists and turns. It helps to have a wicked sense of humor.

If you're lucky, you discover a new, more meaningful friendship in those who "brung you to the dance," if you get my drift. Thank you to my high school pals and best friends forever from the class of 1965 at West Point High School. We are like the Rockettes—all dancing together and leaning on each other when circumstances require it. Together we have survived the passages of time through love and a lot of laughter.

When we're together, the term "aging" takes on a new and exciting meaning. If our mothers could see us behaving so outrageously, we'd be grounded for the rest of our lives. Come join us in our adventures, and let's put off this aging thing as long as possible.

Love, Laughter
&
Losing My Keys

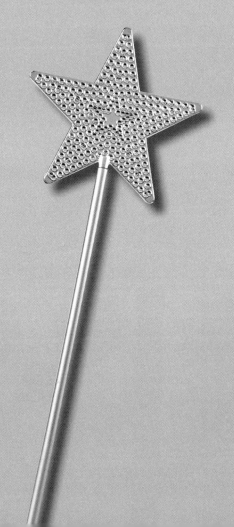

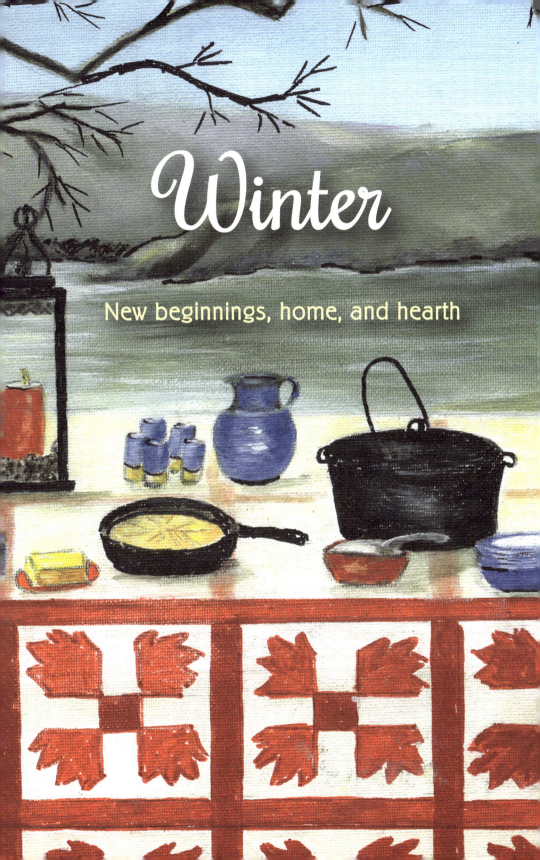

Winter

New beginnings, home, and hearth

Look for God Winks in the New Year

As the holiday season draws to a close, it's time to tame the convivial chaos of the holidays and consume the leftovers which are always better the second time around.

As I attempted to shove some Christmas decorations under my bed, I found a book I bought years ago. It was a delightful little volume which discusses a phenomenon called "God winks." Call them whatever you like—coincidences, kismet—I choose to call them miracles, and they show up often . . . if you're paying attention.

I'm sure you've experienced them. Like when you were nine years old and spilled your chocolate milk all over your grandmother's heirloom tablecloth. Your mother yelled at you and your daddy glared at you while your grandmother sent you a conspiratorial wink that let you know all was right with the world.

God probably does the same thing when we tell a little white lie, and he gives us a mere pang of remorse rather than the flogging we deserve.

God winks are a term coined by Squire Bushnell, a former television network executive who penned *When God Winks* just after the attacks on September 11, 2001. The content relates numerous stories of people who narrowly missed being in the World Trade Center or the Pentagon on that fateful day due to some last-minute distraction that saved their lives.

For example, Chef Michael LoMonaco of Windows on the World restaurant narrowly escaped the September 11 attacks when he accidentally sat on his glasses; on the morning of 9/11 when the first plane plowed into his restaurant, he was at a repair shop waiting for his specs to be repaired.

Many of the stories in the book brought tears to my eyes, but then I cry during Folgers coffee commercials. The stories made me wonder if coincidences even exist at all. I have a friend who met her future husband when she missed her flight out of Atlanta . . . and was bumped off a second flight. She was finally booked on a third flight and assigned to a seat next to an interesting man. Before the flight ended, the two had made plans to meet again, and the rest is history. What if she hadn't missed those first two flights?

Coincidence? I don't think so. I like to think that life's grand plan depends on serendipitous events to help us along the way and to get us back on track when we wander off the rails.

So here's to a New Year packed with good fortune and more God winks than you can count. Now, let's get on with the year by preparing some lucky comfort food.

Mama M's Lucky Cabbage Soup

Everyone knows you must eat cabbage on New Year's Day to ensure good luck and prosperity during the coming year. Here's a spectacular spin on any cabbage recipe you've ever tasted.

1 head cabbage, chopped
2 cups chicken broth
2 ribs celery, diced
1 carrot, diced
1 medium onion, chopped
¼ cup butter (we always use the real thing)
3 tablespoons flour
1 teaspoon salt
⅓ teaspoon pepper
½ teaspoon dried thyme
½ teaspoon parsley
2 cups milk
1 cup whipping cream
2 cups cubed cooked ham (leftover from your Christmas feast)

In a large stockpot, combine first 5 ingredients. Bring to a boil. Reduce heat, cover, and simmer 15–20 minutes until vegetables are tender. Melt butter in a saucepan, add flour and seasonings, and cook to form a paste. Combine cream and milk and gradually add to flour mixture, stirring until thick. Slowly stir cream mixture into vegetables and add ham. Heat thoroughly. Serve with cornbread muffins and savor the compliments.

Warren Buffett dropped in and I liked ta fell out!

Pardon my grammar, but the headline says it best. Words cannot adequately express the degree of embarrassment heaped on me because I'm just a little bit cheap.

For several years I've been a member of an investment club with eleven female friends who are not very big spenders, either. We each kick in $25 a month to buy stocks on the New York Stock Exchange in hopes of someday scoring big in the world of "high finance"—well, make that "low finance."

We buy stock in companies that make things that we use every day—like Kleenex, Vicks Vapor Rub, and Ziploc bags. We meet once a month, with each "partner" rotating as hostess. When it was my turn, I decided to serve my Aunt Emma's Famous Turnip Green Soup. Sounds awful, I know, but it's really quite good, embarrassingly cheap, and a breeze to whip up at a moment's notice.

Each month, we try to get a speaker (someone who knows more than we do about financial matters—pretty much anyone on the planet). Our program chairman called me to say we had a special surprise guest coming to deliver our keynote address at my place.

I vacuumed the house and was about to get out the good china and crystal until I remembered the cute Styrofoam cups I had bought at a local gift shop. They were embossed with the words Redneck Crystal. I thought that would be good for a laugh and would make the perfect vessel in which to serve Aunt Emma's Turnip Green Soup.

Everyone arrived at 6:30 p.m. sharp, and they all seemed unusually excited. While I sprayed air freshener trying to neutralize the smell of turnip greens, someone spilled the beans and announced that Warren Buffett was going to be our special guest.

I was both flabbergasted and mortified! WARREN BUFFETT, the king of Wall Street and the second richest person in the world, was coming to my humble abode? Stock in his company, Berkshire Hathaway, sells for about $100,000 a pop, and I was going to entertain him with soup in a Styrofoam cup?

The doorbell rang. Everyone stampeded to the door, and there stood this distinguished man who seemed genuinely delighted to be visiting in my home . . . at least until Rebel, my nervous Boston terrier, threw up on his Italian loafers. I was speechless and went to find the Windex to clean up his shoes. I was really trying to stall the moment I had to serve this iconic wizard of the financial world my low-country fare.

As I began to dish out the soup, I realized it looked eerily similar to what Rebel had just thrown up on Mr. Buffett's shoes. "Help me," I prayed. "Get me out of this, and I will never be so cheap again."

Just as I was about to have a stroke, the alarm on my clock radio signaled the beginning of a new day. The sound mercifully rescued me from my all-time worst nightmare!

I'm sharing my recipe for all you cheap, lazy socialites of the world. To keep it a secret wouldn't be fair to mankind. It really is delicious, and I've even taken it to tailgates and potlucks—just not when Warren Buffett is in town.

Aunt Emma's Turnip Green Soup

Serve with cornbread muffins unless Warren Buffett is coming to dinner. In that case, you might want to make Yorkshire pudding or something more cosmopolitan.

2–3 (15-ounce) cans turnip greens or mustard greens
2 (15-ounce) cans Ranch-Style Beans with jalapeños
2 potatoes, roughly chopped
2 cans Rotel tomatoes
1 can diced tomatoes
1 meaty ham bone or leftovers from your Christmas ham
   (if you can find some without freezer burn)

Mix all ingredients and cook 4–6 hours in a slow cooker.

No negatives spoken here

I had a huge epiphany as I watched the bowl games on television this year, and it was downright disconcerting.

Who was that person judging and openly criticizing everyone and everything from the football players' hairdos and hideous tattoos to the tasteless TV commercials? Oh, my gosh! It was all coming out of my mouth between scoops of black-eyed pea dip and cabbage au gratin. I sounded to myself like Dolly Parton on helium. Here I was doing everything I could to ensure good fortune in the New Year while tearing the rest of the world to shreds.

This will never do, I told myself. Miss Curmudgeon, you'd better take care of this shortcoming before you lose all your friends. If there was a pageant for Miss Negative America, I would win hands down. What better time than New Year's to turn over a new leaf and stop judging others in a futile attempt to feel superior? I wish I could attribute this negativity to teenage rebellion, but that train left the station a half century ago.

Outwardly, I used to be a pretty nice girl—helpful, polite, never jaywalked or parked in handicapped spaces. I had plenty of friends who liked spending time with me. Now I'm wondering why anyone wants to listen to my constant stream of negative remarks. All this criticism reminds me of a puppy chasing his tail. It's a lot of work for not much reward.

I'm thinking about having a yard sign printed up that says "No Negatives Spoken Here" and planting it in front of my house to hold myself accountable. That way, I'll be too embarrassed to express a negative thought about someone, knowing I'll get busted publicly.

I researched how to change this behavior and learned a simple trick to try if you have a similar problem. When you hear yourself criticizing someone, stop and take a moment to come up with one thing you like about that person. Then praise him or her—out loud. So next time I see a football player sporting long, dangling locks and covered with tattoos, I will say something like "I hope he doesn't get his locks caught in a blender," or "He must have a very high threshold for pain to endure a hot pen carving all those bloody snake dragons onto his skin."

Of course, if the tattoo says "I Love Mom," it's totally okay.

I read somewhere that how we judge others is a reflection of how we judge ourselves. I must be about six inches tall by now after the flogging I've endured over the years. Come to think of it, I complain about my hair on a regular basis. Ergo, I look for bad hair on others and get pretty delighted to find someone who shares my plight. No more.

I have a challenge for you in 2014. Be pretty if you can; be witty if you must; but stop judging others if it kills you.

If you're serving a meal at your bowl game party or New Year's Day party, it's a good idea to serve up one healthy item if you can. My BFE (best friend for eternity) Marie always brings her redneck caviar. It doesn't hurt that the main ingredient is black-eyed peas. Everyone in Mississippi knows you are required to eat black-eyed peas on New Year's or risk an entire year of bad luck.

Marie's Redneck Caviar

1 (15-ounce) can black beans
1 (15-ounce) can field peas
1 (15-ounce) can black-eyed peas
1 (8-ounce) can shoepeg corn
1 (15-ounce) can diced tomatoes, undrained
1 (16-ounce) bottle Zesty Italian Dressing

Drain and rinse black beans, field peas, black-eyed peas and corn and put into large portable container. Add tomatoes and dressing. Gently stir all ingredients and refrigerate overnight to let seasonings blend. Serve with Frito Scoops.

Does housekeeping have roots in Greek mythology?

I have come to the conclusion that housekeeping is about as pointless as rolling a big rock up a hill. Just when you get it to the top, it rolls back down, and you have to do it all over again.

I pondered this idea as I cleaned my house for my Super Bowl Bash. The project was complicated by my 24-year-old Kirby vacuum cleaner, which is way past its prime. Suddenly, with a big belch, it regurgitated everything it had sucked up over the past two months. I turned it upside down to see what the problem might be, and lo and behold, the handle just released itself from the canister at the worst possible time.

Disgusted and figuring I'd gotten my money's worth out of the appliance, I gathered all the parts and took them out to the curb. Maybe some handy person would pick them up and give my Kirby new life.

Now what? Since most of my guests are approaching senior citizenship, I considered asking them to check their eyeglasses at the door. That way they couldn't see the dust balls or the spider web dangling from the dining room chandelier. But no, I dutifully headed out to Lowe's to shop for a new vacuum cleaner.

After about thirty seconds of contemplation, I bought a spiffy model in pond-scum green. That seems to be the new hot color in appliances . . . reminds me of that avocado green from the 70s with a putrid bit of yellow thrown in. I'll be embarrassed by it in two years.

I got it home and spent the next eighteen hours trying to figure out how to assemble it. When my ship comes in, I'm opening a store for people who are challenged by directions written by someone in China. Everything will be already put together and ready to use!

Finally, I got it looking like the picture on the directions and resumed my cleaning marathon.

As its motor hummed and the dust balls piled up in the bagless receptacle, my mind wandered to my college days and my favorite class: Greek mythology.

I compared my plight to the torture of Sisyphus. Do you remember him? He was a sad character who offended Zeus and was sentenced to roll a boulder to the top of a hill for eternity. When he got it to the top, the stone would slide back down again and old Sisy would have to begin the struggle anew.

Cleaning the house is no more than a self-imposed "Sisyphusian" activity. What's the point? I'll just need to do it again in a few days. Flashback: I remember my ten-year old son, William, asking me why he needed to make his bed before going to school. "I'll just muss it up again tonight," he whined. Suddenly it all made sense, and that ten-year-old's reasoning seemed very wise indeed.

But here I go, rolling that rock back up the hill when I could be doing something important like writing the Great American novel. I planned to finish by noon so I could spend the rest of the day engaged in my favorite activity, the subtle art of puttering and piddling. To make sure I'm not distracted from the two activities, I tossed a Boston Butt in the "Crotch Pot" (that's what my friend Kate calls her slow cooker). Tomorrow I will have some delicious pulled pork to serve my guests.

Slow Cooker Barbecue

This is great if you have company coming because it can be made ahead and reheated when you're ready to serve.

1 (5-pound) Boston Butt Roast
Salt and freshly ground pepper to taste
1 cup white vinegar
½ cup firmly packed brown sugar
1 bottle of your favorite barbecue sauce
1 onion, halved

Season roast with salt and pepper. Place in a slow cooker and add vinegar. Cook on HIGH for 1 hour. Turn to LOW and cook overnight or for about 12 hours. Drain and shred roast into pieces. Place meat back in slow cooker. Mix brown sugar and barbecue sauce and pour over meat. Place onion halves on top of meat and cook on low for 2–3 hours.

Parting with my "lucky dress"

As I contemplated the New Year and the sad state of my wardrobe, I bemoaned the fact that I had nothing to wear and certainly no "statement" pieces the designers are always yammering about. January called for a good purging of garments which no longer suited me and probably no longer fit me.

I stood in the middle of my walk-in closet, surrounded by groaning racks of bad choices and ill-advised purchases, and launched the Great January Elimination. Every cotton-picking thing hanging in that closet either scratched, itched, pinched, sagged, or looked just plain dowdy.

What was I thinking when I bought that orange sweater that makes me look jaundiced? And why did I have five identical black turtlenecks?

Then there were the black suede boots I could wear for a maximum of fifteen minutes before tears began to run down my face. I dared to wear them to church one Sunday and everyone around me thought I was having a religious experience. I was, and it was caused by those blasted pointy-toed boots that were created by the devil himself.

I began pulling out every item of clothing I'd unconsciously been resenting. I tossed them in a pile in the middle of the floor and stood back to survey the size of my folly. I angrily estimated what these purchases (impulse for the most part) had cost me in terms of dollars and the guilt that stabs me each time I walk into the closet.

Left hanging were those pitifully few things that offered creature comfort . . . or made me look thin. There wasn't much: my size six jeans which I'm determined to wear by spring; the mint green terrycloth bathrobe with chocolate stains which I'd wear twenty-four hours a day if I could get away with it; a beautiful cashmere sweater that itched but looked so cute hanging there. Oh, and way in the back was my lucky little black dress.

I'd been putting it off for several years, but the time had come to have a talk with that dress. It was at least eighteen years old—I wore it at the height of my career. I'm terribly superstitious, and one day I discovered that when I wore that dress, the world bowed before me. I closed all kinds of deals and obtained approval on every project I pitched while wearing that little black dress.

There really was something magical about the frock, but it had taken on a shiny look, the result of too many visits to the dry cleaners. It was also losing its hem and didn't hang right since I removed the monster shoulder pads.

I reverently removed the dress and tossed it into the pile. After vacuuming the closet and dusting the shelves, I began replacing only those things that I could tolerate. The rest went to my car to be donated to charity. What was left was what one philosopher calls "The Fertile Void"—a big empty space waiting to be filled more creatively than before. It also left me with a space that had more of a boutique feel. I felt free for at least two minutes.

I should have been ecstatic, but something was seriously wrong. I can't explain it, but I had an intense feeling of doom. Then it hit me. My lucky dress was buried under a pile of unlucky apparel in the back of my truck. It didn't deserve such treatment. It had served me well, and one never knew when a situation might arise when that lucky dress would NEED to be mustered into active duty one last time. I rushed out and threw things over my shoulders in what I call an *I Love Lucy* moment.

Oh, thank heavens. There it was—sad and crumpled—but still breathing. I crushed it to my heart and carried it back to the bedroom where I gingerly laid it on the bed. I'd have given it mouth-to-mouth resuscitation if it had a mouth.

I knew in my heart I would never let ole "Blackie" go. Maybe I'd wear her around the house when I needed inspiration. Who knows, she and I might write the Great American Novel after all. To welcome Blackie back home, I set about making my friend Margaret Ann's ultimate comfort food. What else but mac and cheese, the way only Margaret Ann can do it.

Not Ya Mama's Mac & Cheese

1½ cups coarsely grated sharp cheddar cheese (about 6 ounces)

1½ cups coarsely diced Brie cheese with rind removed

1½ cups coarsely grated Gruyere cheese

1 (8-ounce) package cream cheese, softened

5 tablespoons butter, divided

¼ cup all purpose flour

2 teaspoons fresh thyme leaves (better than ground)

¾ teaspoon nutmeg

4 cups whole milk, heated

½ medium onion, chopped and ½ medium bell pepper, chopped and seeded and wilted in 2 tablespoons butter

1 pound penne pasta

Mix all cheeses. Set aside 1 cup for topping. Cover and chill. Melt 4 teaspoons butter in a large saucepan over medium heat. Add flour and stir until mixture turns golden brown (about 4–5 minutes). Add thyme and nutmeg. Gradually stir in heated milk and slowly simmer until thickened and smooth, stirring constantly to keep from sticking. Add cheeses and continue stirring until well melted and very smooth. Fold in wilted onions and peppers.

Cook pasta in boiling water until tender but firm to the bite. Drain well. Transfer to a large bowl and fold in cheese sauce, coating well. Place in large well-greased casserole, or, to be "fancy schmancy," you can pour into individual ramekins or custard cups. Bake at 350° for 30–35 minutes. Top with reserved cheese and sprinkle with bread crumbs (if desired), during last 3 or 4 minutes of baking.

Margaret Ann's Anything Goes Pork Chops

I like to serve Margaret Ann's pork chops with Not Ya Mama's Mac and Cheese.

1 package dry Lipton Onion Soup Mix
6 nice boneless pork chops
1 package dry ranch seasoning mix
1 can cream of chicken soup (plus one can water)

Mix all ingredients well. Margaret Ann always places sliced onions in bottom of the slow cooker. It flavors tremendously, plus they are so tender and good to eat. Cook 4–6 hours until tender.

One of Margaret Ann's variations on this recipe is Hawaiian style pork chops. Add a 16-ounce can chunk pineapple, drained.

You can also add Little Dooey BBQ sauce which Margaret Ann invented and can be purchased at her restaurant (The Little Dooey in Starkville, Mississippi), or if you insist, you can substitute Kraft Catalina or Russian bottled dressing. Place all ingredients in the slow cooker and cook 4–6 hours. Sometimes she adds a big dab of orange marmalade. Margaret Ann can find a way to use just about anything in the fridge and the results are delicious.

My take on the Super Bowl

'm still mulling over the messages delivered by television advertising during the big game on Super Bowl Sunday. It seems to me that television advertising is designed to encourage us to buy things we don't need with money we don't have to impress people we don't even know.

I would do so joyfully if I could identify which products they were pushing.

For me, the Super Bowl stopped being about football a long time ago . . . well, except for that year the Saints finally showed up at the big dance. We'll be talking about that forever. The Super Bowl has become an excuse to consume artery-clogging food and laugh it up at clever commercials, half of which go a foot over my blond head.

The room got quiet as we watched some guy chasing a cheetah chasing a gazelle. At the conclusion, everyone roared gleefully, including my chum, Marie, who was sitting next to me.

"I don't get it," I whispered to her. We were sitting in the back of the room where we could secretly pick the icing off an entire King Cake. I had been on a sugar fast for six weeks and the relapse delivered a buzz equal to a half fifth of Jack Daniels.

"I didn't get it, either," she admitted, but she was still chuckling along with everyone else in the roomful of folks who seemed to get it. But because laughter is so much fun, who cares? So I laughed too—only a little too loudly, and a little too late. Everyone looked at me like I was a dumb blond, a role I have perfected over the years.

Naturally, the most panned commercial was my favorite. It featured a bunch of senior citizens sneaking out of the personal care home to perform some sophomoric pranks, loiter at a fast food restaurant, and party down at a night club.

Ah, what memories flooded my mind. I recalled climbing out of my dorm room at Ole Miss more than four decades ago and having the time of my life. It was heartwarming to know I can have those times again when my children plunk me into the home.

On sleepless nights, I'll be the one to grab my Hurry Cane, climb out the window, and steal an old Plymouth to go joyriding. Once, long ago, we drove our parents crazy, and now it is payback time for our children. Thank you, Mr. Unknown Advertiser, for reminding me that crazy wicked fun isn't reserved for the young.

Most of the ads left me cold. But to tell the truth, I had

forgotten my glasses and could see only a big blur on the screen. Paul Harvey did get my attention when the radio host delivered a poignant ode to the American farmer. I'm not sure what he was advertising, but our farmers got a well-earned and overdue plug and I got a lump in my throat.

My biggest regret is that I missed *Masterpiece Theatre*, which the Super Bowl had the gall to eclipse. Everyone knows that men rule the remote, and an English epic didn't stand a chance against a testosterone overload and hot wings.

Here's the easiest recipe I've ever had the pleasure of throwing together. It was given to me by Lisa McReynolds, who named it Doo Doo Dip. I think it will sound more appetizing if you call it Voodoo Dip.

Lisa's World Famous Doo Doo Dip

Lisa usually cooks this on the stove-top over medium heat and then throws it all in a slow cooker to keep it warm for the party.

1 can of regular chili (with or without beans, your choice)
1 can of chili, labeled "hot"
2 (8-ounce) packages cream cheese, softened
1 (8-ounce) package regular Velveeta cheese
1 (8-ounce) package Mexican Velveeta cheese

Combine all ingredients, heat, and serve with Fritos Scoops or tortilla chips, your choice! Try adding some sour cream or jalapeños and hot sauce for garnish.

Illegally blond

Yesterday I began mulling over the possibility of going "au naturel." Just the hair, you understand. All other things false will continue as long as I can remember what's real.

Next week, I reach an unthinkable age. The one where you get to partake of that masterful government program called Medicare. How did that happen? Yesterday I was a swinging single, dating dashing young men, and now I'm perusing the ads for corrective shoes and fortified oatmeal. All the dashing young men in my life are renting the house next door.

Time is such a fickle friend. You can't wait to grow up; when you do, you're too busy to enjoy it. Then, overnight, you become a senior citizen and don't even feel like taking advantage of all those enticing senior discounts. You just want to stay home and wait for *Wheel of Fortune* to come on your new high definition television set, which you never learned to program so you could tape the show and watch it late at night when insomnia sets in.

Even the definition of late has changed. Once it was two a.m. Now it's more like nine p.m.

Wait a minute. No, I'm not going down that road just yet. So I renewed my gym dues and booked a facial at the spa. I bought some four-inch stilettos and a subscription to *Cosmo*. Not that I'll ever enjoy any of these things, but they will look good on the coffee table. I went out and bought a filmy negligee and keep it hanging on the headboard . . . just in case.

Old age only matters if you are a cheese or a bottle of wine.

But back to my hair. The girls of the Class of 1965 from West Point High School agreed that we would all go gray together, and they keep moving it back each year. I was computing what I could do with all the savings I'd rack up by giving up the hair color. Six professional colors and cuts a year would add up to a Mediterranean cruise or some plastic surgery.

As it turns out, a bout with cancer gave me the perfect solution. All my hair fell out; I got a couple of fabulous wigs; if the hair ever comes back, I'm never coloring it again. For some reason all this reminds me of my friend, Beth Hooker Herron, who has great hair and is the most self-confident girl I know—even if she WAS a Hooker before she married Charles (in name only, of course). Her brisket is so good it should be illegal.

Beth's Brisket

This is great to prepare in advance and take on a road trip or to the ballpark. You may want to serve as a main meat dish or serve on a hoagie bun or sandwich bread. Even better, serve slices on Judy Murphy Stagger's To Die For Biscuits (see next page).

1 (4-ounce) bottle Liquid Smoke
½ teaspoon celery salt
½ teaspoon garlic salt or powder
½ teaspoon onion salt or powder
½ teaspoon seasoned salt
½ teaspoon pepper
2 tablespoons Worcestershire sauce
1 medium (5–6 pound) beef brisket, remove visible fat
   with an electric knife
1 cup barbecue sauce, your choice

For marinade, mix all ingredients except brisket and barbecue sauce in a bowl. Place the brisket on heavy duty foil (it is best to double your foil). Pour the marinade over brisket and seal tightly. Place in fridge and marinate at least 24 hours. Place the tightly-sealed brisket in preheated 250° oven and bake for 5 hours. After 5 hours, open the foil and pour your favorite barbecue sauce over the brisket. Do not reseal the foil. Return to oven and bake 1 additional hour. Let the brisket cool completely before slicing or you may return to fridge and slice later.

Judy's To Die For Biscuits

2 cups Bisquick
⅔ cups milk
½ cup grated sharp Cheddar cheese
½ cup melted butter
½ teaspoon garlic salt

Mix Bisquick, milk, and Cheddar cheese until a soft ball forms. Beat vigorously for 30 seconds or so. Drop balls onto parchment-lined baking sheet and bake at 450° for 8–10 minutes. Mix melted butter and garlic salt and generously brush on biscuits while still on the pan and hot.

Judy's notes: (I love it when cooks tell you the little secrets.) Judy always uses 2% milk for EVERYTHING! She uses a melon ball scoop or just uses 2 teaspoons–one that holds the dough, and the other to push it off the spoon onto the cookie sheet.

Using parchment paper IS A MUST! Otherwise, the biscuits may stick to the pan or brown on the bottom too much. This "sticking" happened to her while making biscuits for 75 at a church lunch a while back. (Talk about embarrassment!)

These are best served right out of the oven. Don't mix up the dough too early or it'll dry out. Judy always has the Bisquick and cheese in the bowl and is ready to add the milk at the last minute. Combine the butter and garlic salt in a small, covered saucepan to have it ready to "drown" the hot biscuits! Keep it warm, but be careful not to burn the butter!

Laughter really is the best medicine

"What's the funniest thing that has happened to you this week?"

That's the way most conversations begin during a reunion of my high school friends who live close enough to get together at least once a month for some laughter therapy. We don't really plan it as "medicinal," but the feeling of total relaxation after we whoop it up for an afternoon is a testament to the stress-reducing properties of laughter.

We guffaw in the most unladylike manner as we recall our friend who accidentally swallowed her hearing aid battery instead of her osteoporosis pill. Another dropped a contact lens into the potato salad at a church picnic and it was never found.

We collapse onto the floor laughing about our hometown

friend who grabbed a jacket out of his garage to attend a fancy cocktail party. At the party someone asked if he knew he had a dirt dauber nest hanging on his sleeve. *Hardy har har.* That same friend accidentally maced himself while driving a borrowed car. He thought the innocuous little can on the passenger seat was breath spray. *Giggle, snort.* Oh, and what about the time he had to drive his riding lawnmower to church because his children had taken all the cars? By now we are in tears.

Let's face it, life can be pretty funny. These stories are valuable little gems we carry in our memories to be pulled up when the world threatens to beat us down. And each time we get together, we get to add new "stupid people tricks" to our repertoire.

You've probably heard about American journalist Norman Cousins, who came down with a fatal illness and was given one month to live. He checked out of the hospital and into a hotel where he treated himself with mega-doses of Vitamin C, chased by hours of laughter induced by old Marx Brothers films. He discovered that ten minutes of genuine belly laughter had a healing anesthetic effect and would give him at least two hours of pain-free sleep. Long story short, he went on to live for twenty-six more years.

Laughter is that delicious sound that occurs involuntarily and bubbles from deep in your soul. It can leave you breathless and relaxed. I wish someone would package it.

Look, we have figured out how to split the atom to the nth degree, put men on the moon, and mapped our DNA . . . but no one has figured out how to give us laughter on demand? Personally, I always get a kick out of *America's Funniest Videos*. With Rebel and Lucky Dawg at my side we laugh hysterically—even Rebel, who is a bulldog with a perpetual scowl. We especially love the clips involving pets, small children, and people falling down at their weddings.

Be forewarned, laughter is highly contagious and can add years to your life. I guess that makes us about 125 by now.

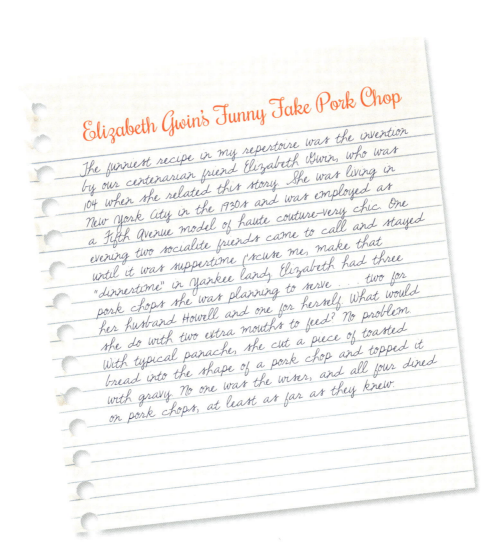

Elizabeth Gwin's Funny Fake Pork Chop

The funniest recipe in my repertoire was the invention by our centenarian friend Elizabeth Gwin, who was 104 when she related this story. She was living in New York City in the 1930s and was employed as a Fifth Avenue model of haute couture—very chic. One evening two socialite friends came to call and stayed until it was suppertime ('scuse me, make that "dinnertime" in Yankee land). Elizabeth had three pork chops she was planning to serve . . . two for her husband Howell and one for herself. What would she do with two extra mouths to feed? No problem. With typical panache, she cut a piece of toasted bread into the shape of a pork chop and topped it with gravy. No one was the wiser, and all four dined on pork chops, at least as far as they knew.

Desperate housewife puzzles over unsolved mysteries

I'm not exactly a housewife, but I do consider myself a desperate housekeeper these days. Since I retired, I've been trying to hone my latent domestic skills. I'm increasingly puzzled and dismayed by recurring situations that threaten to drive me screaming into the streets.

I can't begin to understand the complexities of the universe, and I'm ever amazed and impressed with how far mankind has come in making our lives more comfortable. Yet I feel technology has failed housewives everywhere by not address-ing some universal conundrums.

For example, how can I keep Mr. Coffee from dribbling all over my shoes every time I attempt a caffeine infusion? I'm a big coffee drinker, and I figure that I've lost several hundred gallons of coffee through that mysterious leak that occurs around the lip of the carafe regardless of how carefully and slowly I pour.

You'd think some mastermind of the small appliance world would have solved such dilemmas by now. Then, lo and behold, I broke Mr. Coffee's glass carafe the other day, which served him right after all the angst he's caused. Believe it or not, a replacement pot was cruelly priced to be more expensive than replacing the entire coffee maker!

It was cheaper for me to buy a new caffeine maker. My exhaustive search for a dripless model was futile. After driving to three cities in search of the newest generation of coffee machines, I ended up buying an expensive (albeit handsome) appliance that looked way too sophisticated to dribble. I couldn't wait to get it home and try it out.

I have renamed the new pot Mr. Niagara Falls because he leaks worse than the late Mr. Coffee. While I'm on the subject of these unruly men living in my house, I also have a beef with Mr. Clean, who fails miserably in his promise to keep a tidy house. Does anyone have an explanation for the sticky substance that forms on the bottom of every jar in the refrigerator, even the ones that have never been opened? As I cleaned out the fridge this weekend, about half the jars were stuck like cement to the shelves, rendering Mr. Clean totally impotent. What's that about?

I began to think about all the other household mysteries I've encountered recently and suspect my house is haunted. Who has absconded with my favorite writing pens? I buy a dozen at a time and they are all gone! And what about the ongoing mystery of the hijacked socks? Oh, yeah—the dryer is evil. I washed a load of dark clothes with three pairs of socks yesterday. Three sad socks emerged without mates. That pesky bottle of Mr. Clean hovering above the dryer caught my eye and he was beginning to look guilty as sin.

"Hey, Mr. Clean, what'd you do with my socks? Yo, Mr. Clean! I'm talkin' to you, you worthless household helper!"

Desperate housewives looking for effortless ways to get dinner on the table will want to try my Crispy Onion Chicken:

Crispy Onion Chicken

Chicken breasts (probably 1 or 2 for empty nesters)
1-2 tablespoons prepared mustard
Canned onion rings, crushed

Brush boneless chicken breasts on all sides with mustard. Roll in crushed onion rings. Bake at 350° for 20 minutes. Voila ... dinner is served.

New fragrance: Essence of burned popcorn

Let me tell you about the breakup of my family—the folks I spend time with on a daily basis.

First there's Cousin Willie and his sidekick, Mrs. Dash. We typically watch the news together every evening. Cousin Willie is my favorite brand of microwave popcorn, and Mrs. Dash gives the cuz a bit of a kick. Unfortunately we're not getting along these days.

It all started about three weeks ago. My specs were at the other end of the kitchen when I popped Cousin Willie into the microwave. I squinted at the dial and punched what I thought was the popcorn button and shuffled outside to see how my pansies were percolating.

Ten minutes later, upon entering the house with visions of

settling down with a big bowl of fluffy popcorn and the evening news, I was almost knocked down by a foul odor. Thick billows of smoke were churning throughout the space, and the smell would have killed a herd of pigs. Rebel and Lucky Dawg were rolling on the floor covering their noses with their paws.

The only thing I can figure is that I must have pressed the baked potato button, which is one row above the popcorn command and about ten times as many minutes on high.

Is there any smell worse than burned popcorn? Even though I cleaned the soot off the inside of the oven, everything in the house continues to reek of burned popcorn. When I reheat my coffee, it tastes of burned popcorn, and my home now has tinted windows which I got free of charge.

When I dropped in to visit my neighbor, she took a whiff and said, "Been burning popcorn, have you?"

I went online to get some tips on neutralizing the odor. You can put half a cup of lemon juice and half a cup of water in a four-cup microwave-safe container and cook on high until the water boils and creates steam. The steam will help eliminate the lingering odor. If the smell is really stubborn, you may need to follow up with some baking soda on a damp sponge and scrub the interior surfaces of the microwave.

I'm still estranged from Cousin Willie and Mrs. Dash. I carry with me the vivid memory of that olfactory assault on my senses. It has blunted my taste buds and given me a phobia-like fear of cooking popcorn.

Here's a sweet idea to zing up your taste buds while Willie and old lady Dash cool their heels. It's as easy as microwave popcorn!

Chocolate-dipped Pretzel Rods

½ cup chocolate chips
Pretzel rods

Melt chocolate chips in microwave. Dip rods in melted chocolate, and let cool on wax paper. Done!

Spring

Everything old is new again

Living perfectly in an imperfect world

I read somewhere that one of the most direct roads to happiness is to develop the ability to see the positive aspects of those things which, at first glance, may appear to be negatives.

Boy, am I familiar with negatives! They seem to be multiplying like rabbits at my house. I can't get my bank statement to balance, the kitchen sink has developed a slow drip, and the Christmas decorations still clutter the guest room. They are waiting patiently and annoyingly to be taken to the attic. Can't anyone around here do something for themselves?

To make things worse, I wandered around the garden at dawn to observe what perennials might be poking through. Some kind of thorny vine seems to have taken over the landscape. My porch lights are so dusty you can hardly tell there's a light bulb inside, and there's a green slime growing on the house. I think they call it mildew, and I'm feeling a little green myself from winter's cabin fever.

In an effort to gain some kind of control, I sit down and make a list of all the spring cleaning chores that need doing. It takes two pages. I am so overwhelmed I want to go back to bed and pull the covers over my head.

But no, I tell myself. Be strong and take one chore each day and work on it for at least thirty minutes. Baby steps, sure, but maybe in a couple of months the place won't look so ragged.

Do we ever find a modicum of perfection in our lives? Perhaps without the imperfect, we wouldn't be able to appreciate those perfect moments in our lives. Would we ever have a good hair day if we had never had a bad hair day? I wouldn't know because I'm still waiting on a good hair day.

Some people insist we can find beauty hidden within the imperfections of life. Think about the Mona Lisa's crooked smile, the Leaning Tower of Pisa, or the pain of giving birth (which produces new life). Imperfection CAN be a beautiful thing.

Right now I'm gazing at a fire-ant bed under construction and trying to assign it some positive quality. I'm drawing a blank.

I'd rather have an administrative assistant to take care of all my chores, but what purpose would our lives have if we lacked the spunk to correct those imperfections? Life would eventually get pretty boring if everything was perfect, or so they say.

If we had no home improvement projects to excite us, no closets to clean out and refresh us, or no kitchens to clean up before we get them dirty again, what would we do?

Simply put, imperfections add purpose to our lives. Without the glitches, we would have nothing to reach for on life's journey. At least, this is the message I'm trying to ram through my own skull, and it's giving me a splitting headache.

Today, I'll tackle the Christmas decorations. Then again, it's only nine months until I'll need them again. I think I'll just let them live in the guest room this year—I won't even need to change the sheets.

I read somewhere that as machines and technology enable us to become more efficient, it will become clear that the imperfection of man is what makes him human. That said, the writer was talking about men. He didn't say a thing about women.

Speaking of perfection, my friend since second grade—Ruthie Stafford Weathers—shared her recipe for the easiest banana pudding recipe known to men AND women. She knows I despise bananas, but I make this dessert when I'm on a diet and don't want to be tempted. I just can't get past those icky stringy things on the fruit.

Perfect Banana Pudding

Ruthie takes this to all family gatherings. She suspects they wouldn't care if she comes or not, but she must send the pudding.

1 large package instant vanilla pudding mix
3 cups cold milk
1 can Eagle Brand sweetened condensed milk
1 (8-ounce) container Cool Whip
1 box vanilla wafers
5 or 6 bananas, sliced

Using a wire whisk, combine pudding mix, milk, sweetened condensed milk, and Cool Whip. Layer vanilla wafers and sliced bananas in a trifle bowl. Spoon pudding mixture over each layer (makes 2 or 3 layers depending on size of serving dish). Refrigerate for at least 1 hour before serving. Garnish with more cookies, if desired.

The missing casserole caper

It's official. I've finally gone and lost it—my mind, that is. It just up and left me all of a sudden and I'm still reeling from a vapid feeling.

It started when a friend of mine from California came to town for a visit and I invited her over for lunch. Since she's way out on the west coast, she hasn't gotten wind of my culinary disasters and didn't even hesitate to accept my invitation the way my local friends do.

So I spent yesterday cooking and cleaning the house, and put together my vegetarian pasta salad which has become my go-to dish when company comes. It's got whole wheat squiggly pasta shells and every vegetable under the sun, all tossed together with mustard balsamic vinaigrette.

It's pretty good if I do say so myself. It even gets better with age, which has become the guiding principle of my existence here on planet Earth. Doesn't everything get better with age? I say that only because I recently qualified for that exclusive society known as the "elderly." (I can use the "e" word, but you'd best not if you value your health and safety.)

Anyway, I prepared the salad the night before the luncheon so it could marinate a bit. I also prepared sourdough crostinis and a cold squash soup. I named them Squash Martinis only because I serve the soup in martini glasses I picked up at the Dollar Tree for a buck apiece. It raises the lowly crookneck squash to a new level.

One hour before Anne was to arrive, I opened the fridge to remove the salad and let it come to room temperature. BIG problem: there was no pasta salad in the fridge. I rushed around the kitchen shouting "Where is it? Who took my pasta salad?"

Rebel and Lucky Dawg are my only two roommates and if they knew where it went, they weren't saying. In fact, I'm pretty sure Lucky was giggling with glee as I flew into a panic. I rushed through every room in the house—no salad.

There was only one possibility. Oh, please not that . . . I opened the cabinet, and there it was, sitting on top of a stack of casserole dishes like someone put it there on purpose. So, I had a big decision to make. Do I serve a dish which has been sitting in a cabinet all night to my innocent unsuspecting friend, or do I put it down the garbage disposal and go pick up a pizza?

I'm not saying what I did, and you can leave that to your imagination. I will tell you I spoke with my California friend on the phone today and she is alive and well back in L.A. She didn't mention anything about being sick. I was telling my son Braddock about the caper and he volunteered to do the food for my annual Easter brunch. See how that works? I bet no one ever asks me to bring a dish to a potluck again. Works for me.

You must try my Squash Martinis, which make a nice appetizer for a spring brunch.

Squash Martinis

1 small onion, minced
1 clove garlic, minced
3 tablespoons butter
1½ pounds yellow squash, diced
1 (10¾-ounce) can chicken broth
⅔ cup water
½ cup half-and-half (I actually use low-fat sour cream—it's just as good)
¼ teaspoon white pepper
Chopped parsley for garnish

Sauté onion and garlic in butter. Stir in squash, broth, and water and cook until squash is tender. Spoon into blender and process until smooth. Return to pan and add cream (or sour cream) and pepper. Cook over low heat, stirring constantly until well-blended.

Serve chilled in martini glasses or goblets. Best to make ahead because soup improves in flavor as it chills. This will serve 5-6 depending on size of your glasses. I like to garnish the glass with a slice of squash cut halfway through and riding on the rim.

Kitchen Cabinet Casserole

My new name for pasta salad after I left it in the cabinet overnight and tore the house apart looking for it.

DRESSING:
¼ cup balsamic vinegar
4–5 cloves garlic, roughly chopped
1½ teaspoon chili powder
1 teaspoon cumin
½ teaspoon kosher or sea salt
½ cup olive oil
½ cup roughly chopped cilantro (optional)

Mix together dressing ingredients and set aside:

½ pound bowtie or penne pasta
1 (14-ounce) can black beans, drained and rinsed
2 roma tomatoes, diced or about ¾ cup halved cherry tomatoes
1 large red, yellow, or orange bell pepper, diced
½ cup sliced green onions
½ cup frozen or fresh corn kernels (no need to thaw)
Zest from 2 limes
½ cup feta cheese

Boil pasta in salted water according to package directions. Drain, and rinse immediately with cold water. Place in a large salad bowl. Add beans, tomatoes, bell pepper, green onions, corn, and lime zest. Toss with dressing. Add additional salt and pepper to taste. Chill at least 1 hour. Right before serving, sprinkle cheese on top.

Death by cobbler

I've come to realize that family members who can cook delicious dishes are a serious threat to the health of their "kin."

After swearing off sugar for two weeks and dropping five pounds almost immediately, I hit a bump in the road. It was a big bump called "the family reunion." Ironically, I was losing weight to look good for the reunion, which was instrumental in causing me to put it all back on in a matter of minutes!

My cud'n (that's what they're called in Tippah County where my daddy grew up), Becky Braddock Benson, is famous for her unusual "to die for" pot luck offerings. It's always some dish I've never heard of or spotted in one of my more than six dozen cookbooks.

As usual, the traditional reunion potluck included fifteen kinds of fried chicken from Aunt Emma's to Colonel Sanders' and macaroni and cheese prepared every which way but loose.

I casually perused the dessert table. I wasn't partaking, mind you. I'd managed to avoid the sweet stuff for two weeks, and nothing this side of heaven was going to tempt me. No way.

Then I spotted something that looked so enticing my mouth began to water. It looked like a head-on collision between a strudel and a caramel sauce. I figured it would be just awful, so I took a wee taste—just to see if I could identify it. I almost passed out. Oh, my gosh! Was this the best thing I had ever tasted? Or were my poor, sugar-deprived taste buds playing tricks on me?

"Who made this and what is it?" I shouted between mouthfuls of the heavenly concoction. By then I was cleaning the remains of the dish with a spatula I'd pilfered from the green bean casserole. There, in the front row, Becky smiled sweetly and half raised her hand. I should have known. She wins again. I grabbed her by the arm and pulled her into the kitchen.

"I HAVE to have this recipe," I demanded, blocking her escape with a ten-gallon trash can. I grabbed a napkin, gave her a pen, and asked her to write it down. With a drumstick in one hand and the pen in the other, she obliged.

Becky calls it Caramel Cobbler, and I was amazed how simple it is to make. Even better, it calls for things you typically have in the kitchen anyway, and all it takes is one measly dish in which to mix, bake, and serve.

Amazing Magical Tippah County Caramel Cobbler

1 stick butter
1½ cups flour
1½ cups sugar
¾ cup milk
1 teaspoon vanilla
1½ cups brown sugar
Chopped pecans
1½ cups hot water

Melt butter in your serving dish. Becky used a casserole dish approximately 7x11 inches. Mix flour, sugar, milk, and vanilla, and pour on butter. Do not stir. Sprinkle brown sugar and pecans on top . . . and do not stir. Pour water on top. Bake at 350° for 35 minutes. Voila! Dessert is served unless your oven decides to blow up after ten minutes.

Read on for the rest of the cobbler story . . .

failure: just another way of doing things

(A sequel to the previous chapter about Cousin Becky's Caramel Cobbler.)

It's all my cousin's fault. She's a fabulous cook, and over the years I've obtained some special recipes from her. None ever turns out like hers, which makes me suspect she is leaving something critical out of the list of ingredients.

That's exactly why I've been holding off making her famous caramel cobbler. I just couldn't bear to mess this one up. Deep in my heart I knew I would. But the weather was coolish one early spring day and I decided that cobbler would be the perfect way to entertain my college roommate, who was in town for a few days.

I swallowed my fear and carefully measured all the ingredients into little bowls like the TV chefs do. I began to mix things very carefully, following the directions to the "T." (Obviously my "T" is different from my cousin's. What's a "T" anyway?)

I cranked up the old GE to 350 degrees as the recipe specified. After ten minutes into the cooking phase everything was going swimmingly. Wonderful smells were wafting through the house, and I was rehearsing how I would respond to all the kudos when I served it to my friends.

Suddenly I heard something that sounded like a squirrel being electrocuted as he scampered along a live wire. I know that sound well because I watched it happen recently. At first I thought I was cooking something metal in the microwave, then realized with horror that the hair-raising sound was coming from inside the oven . . . where my precious caramel cobbler was percolating.

I opened the door to peek inside, and a ball of fire was circulating around the lower element of the oven. Fiddlesticks. I PROMISED the girls that cobbler, so I did what I always do when crises strike. I called my neighbor, Brenda, and she let me put the cobbler into her oven. I went back thirty minutes later to take it out per the instructions. Brenda noted that it was kind of "sloshy."

I figured the cobbler would take some time cooling its heels on the counter to set up properly. So I hauled it back home, sloshing it on my shoes and leaving a trail from Brenda's side door to my own. It sat all the way through three reruns of *Murder She Wrote* and grew soupier by the moment. Maybe I could serve it in silver goblets and call it an after-dinner drink.

I sealed my fate by sticking it back inside my wounded

oven in an attempt to cook it a little more. With the lower element out of commission, it was simply being broiled. Of course, the sugar on top burned to a deep chocolate brown.

As I dumped the whole thing down the drain, I mulled over yet another culinary failure. The only thing I could do was throw a raincoat over my pajamas and run to the Piggly Wiggly to pick up an Edwards Key Lime Pie. I wish I had done that in the first place, but I harbor this vision of producing something edible and delicious from my cursed kitchen.

I guess cobbler doesn't like being cooked in installments. The good news is that I found a website on how to repair a burned-out oven element. Dare I try? Probably not. I'll cut my losses and limit my oven usage to toast until I can get in touch with my repairman, who visits more often than my family.

Here's another way to doing things that is guaranteed to succeed. It was served to us by our high school friend Carole when we visited on her houseboat in Austin, Texas. This is perfect for a spring brunch accompanied by whatever condiments (fillings) float your boat. Best of all, everyone makes their own.

Do It Yourself Ziploc Omelet

The hostess's dream.

2 eggs per person
Chopped ham
Shredded Cheddar cheese
Chopped onion (green is pretty)
Chopped green and/or red bell pepper
Chopped fresh tomato
Chunky salsa
Fresh mushrooms, chopped
Crisp bacon, crumbled

Have each person crack two eggs into a quart-sized resealable freezer bag such as Ziploc. Press out most of the air, and seal. Shake or squeeze to beat the eggs. Open the bag and add the condiments of choice (approximately 1 tablespoon of each). Shake bag to mix all together. Squeeze out as much of the air as you can, and reseal the bag. (Carole's note: write each person's name on the bag with permanent marker.)

Bring a large pot of water to a boil. Place up to 8 bags at a time into the boiling water. Cook for exactly 13 minutes. Open the bag, and let the omelet roll out onto a plate. The omelet will roll out easily, and it will be perfectly-formed. It's magic.

Will the "real" girl please stand up?

Yesterday an old high school boyfriend told me that he has always enjoyed my company because I was so "real." What does that mean? Is it a put-down or a come-on?

I don't have a clue, but I batted my false eyelashes sweetly, straightened my new wig, checked my makeup in his rear view mirror and replied "Why, thank you!"

My inner voice was shouting "Real WHAT?" Real ugly, real pretty, real phony—real what, pray tell? Exactly what does it mean to be real?

If truth be told, the only "real" time of my day is when I wake up in the morning. Now that's "real," and trust me, it's not pretty.

I have Choctaw blood coursing through my veins (from my

great great grandmother on my Daddy's side), and I'm never really comfortable without my "war paint." I paint on my eyebrows before going out to pick up the newspaper, and keep a lipstick in my pocket for regular touch-ups.

The older I get, the longer it takes to look "real," and it galls me that men get by with so little effort.

But I'm wondering. Is anyone really "real" these days? Nonstop advertising assaults us with all kinds of options to cover our blemishes and present a more attractive package to the world. There are treatments to diminish our flaws and surgeries to augment our "deficiencies."

Brave is the soul who slogs through life without enhancement of some sort. I think we should declare a national holiday called "Get Real Day," where everyone presents his or her true self to the world—warts, halos, and all. On second thought, that could be pretty scary.

So, what does it really mean to be real? Are our instincts dulled from years of trying to mold ourselves into a package acceptable to our human culture? Learning to play more, being more open and less pretentious, re-discovering and cultivating a sense of awe and wonder about life, and losing a little self-importance might be the keys to becoming "real."

Next time you want to compliment someone and can't find a single thing to admire . . .

just tell her that she is "real." It'll make her feel good until she tries to figure out what it means.

Real or unreal, you've GOT to try Margaret Ann's recipe for Zucchini Imperial. Your guests will think you're serving crabmeat but it's really zucchini. Unreal, huh?

Zucchini Imperial
(AKA Faux Crabmeat Casserole)

4 cups sliced zucchini

2 eggs

1 cup mayonnaise

1 medium yellow onion chopped

¼ cup bell pepper chopped

1 cup grated Monterey Jack Cheese

Salt and pepper to taste

1 sleeve Ritz Crackers, crushed

½ stick butter, melted

Boil zucchini until tender in salted water, and drain well. In a large bowl, beat eggs, then add mayo, onion, bell pepper, cheese, seasonings, and cooked zucchini. Mix well. Place in greased 2-quart casserole. Sprinkle cracker crumbs on top, and drizzle with melted butter. Bake at 350° for 30 minutes until bubbly.

Comfort food deficiency
is miserable

Something important has been missing from my life, and for days I've been pondering what has sent me to the far edge of my questionable sanity. Then, lo and behold, it came to me as I was lunching with a friend at a trendy cafe in my hometown.

I sat glaring at the plate of my dining companion and felt an inexplicable anger toward her, the table, and the entire world. The waiter had just delivered her lunch, which was the most decadent work of culinary art I ever feasted my feverish eyes upon. Country fried pork chops were swimming in a pool of white gravy. Black-eyed peas were staring back at me with a "come hither" look. Was that real bacon tucked amongst the peas? They were cozied up to a seductive cloud of fluffy white mashed potatoes daring me to dive in without a life preserver. The plate was punctuated with a cornbread muffin for which I would have given my right hand—and I'm right-handed!

Adding insult to injury, my friend had ordered a side of sweet potato fries which the Cafe Ritz does like no one else. So crispy and salty, they made my hair tingle even though I don't have any hair to speak of, thanks to what I've begun calling my "chemo-cut." I felt like an amputee who says they still feel pain in the missing limb.

Then came my plate. It was an anemic green salad of naked lettuce and a couple of cherry tomatoes. I think there was a mushroom and a celery leaf but I can't be sure. A sudden rage made me want to throw back the table and scream at the top of my lungs: NO. MORE. LETTUCE!

In an instant I knew the source of my fury. I was suffering from a severe case of comfort food deficiency. I wanted meat—real meat—not the fake soy patties I'd been eating on a light bun with lettuce, onion, and cheese and pretending it tasted like a hamburger. I wanted real cheese, not the rubbery, fat-free stuff that tastes like a pencil eraser. I wanted sugar, straight out of a five-pound sack if possible.

For seven months (almost to the day) I'd been wandering around in a comfort food desert, opting for a vegetarian existence featuring raw broccoli, cauliflower, black bean burgers, and kale—which I dutifully choked down and told everyone how delicious it was. Well, I fibbed. It tastes like the leaves on my native azalea.

All this was an experiment to see if a plant-based diet would help cure the cancer. The day before, I had my annual physical and the numbers were so phenomenal my doctor complimented me on being so healthy. Well, Doc, I may be healthy, but I'm far from a happy camper. A girl just needs her meat and three every once in a while.

But back to my luncheon. For revenge, I ate the entire plate of fries and stopped off at the West Point Walmart for a bag of fried chicken fingers the size of Paul Bunyan's digits (which I consumed in the car on the way home). I glanced into the rear view mirror and was horrified to find grease on my nose and in my fake hair; I was in fried chicken heaven and completely out of control. I stopped off at The Little Dooey—conveniently located a block from my house—and picked up a rack of ribs. As long as I was going off my plant-based cancer diet, I was determined to make it memorable.

As if the angels agreed, I arrived home to find my friends, Larry and Mary Bell, on my doorstep with a monstrous, mile-high coconut pie they had picked up at the Crystal Grill in Greenwood. If you've never had a pie from Crystal Grill, you have missed out on the eighth wonder of the world.

The moral of this story is this: Never go for long without your comfort food. Life is too short to miss out on the glories of food like your grandmother made. It is so comforting, so nourishing of body and soul, that eating it is like arriving home after a long journey. Comfort food reminds us that there is a special place to recharge the spirit when it becomes weary of a world complicated by war and pestilence. Who can possibly be uncomfortable while eating a plate of mashed potatoes or Norma's Pineapple Blueberry Cobbler?

Norma's Pineapple Blueberry Dump Cobbler

1 can blueberry pie filling
1 (20-ounce) can crushed pineapple
1 box yellow cake mix
1½ sticks butter, melted

Spray a 9x13-inch pan with Pam. Pour pineapple in pan, and spread around. Pour blueberry pie filling over pineapple, spreading around a bit. Sprinkle dry cake mix over all. Pour butter over top. Bake at 350° for 45 minutes.

Since the sneaky food companies have begun reducing the size of cake mixes by a couple of ounces, Norma says you might want to drain pineapple ever so slightly so it won't be runny.

Burning bush experience on Good Friday

This is beyond weird even for me. At three a.m. on Good Friday, I was awakened by three policemen who were banging on the front door and shining lights into my front parlor.

I stumbled out of bed and, after seeing they were police officers, I opened the door. Policeman Number One said politely, as if he was there to borrow a cup of sugar, "Did you know your flower bed is on fire?"

Sure, I thought. I like to set beds on fire in the middle of the night. Did I look like a pyromaniac, for heaven's sake? But I probably did, in my current state of bed-head, wearing my T-shirt that read "My goal in life is to have a psychiatric disorder named for me."

I peered around the corner and, sure enough, the bed was

shooting flames into the sky while Policeman Number Two sprayed it with my garden hose and Policewoman Number One examined the surrounding area for evidence of arson.

"Gee whiz, I must have really made someone mad," I thought. What really burned me up (no pun intended) is that the bed contained my treasured pass-along hot pink daylilies and red cannas that were preparing for a stunning summer show of color. It usually takes perennials three years before they really shine. This would have been their year.

I wondered what all this meant. Was it a case of spontaneous combustion? A sign from heaven on Good Friday? Did someone throw out a cigarette and it landed on something flammable? I could not imagine.

Through it all, Smirk, my new stray cat, sat calmly on the front porch rocker. (I named her Smirk because she has a black spot on the left side of her mouth and permanently looks as if she has a smirk on her face.)

Smirk knew what really happened, but she was not telling. I didn't have time to dwell on the conundrum because Easter Dinner needed fixin' and I had my kitchen armed and loaded for a huge feast.

No Easter family dinner would be complete without asparagus. Just in case you can't find nice fresh ones, try Norma's Easy Asparagus Congealed Salad or Olivia's Extended Life Tomato Salad, which can live in the fridge into the next century. Olivia got the recipe from Renee Taylor . . . who got it from Ginger DeWeese . . . who got it from Susie Owings . . . and on and on. A recipe can circulate through my entire community on a Sunday afternoon between naps.

Olivia's Extended Life Tomato Salad

¾ cup vegetable oil
¾ cup sugar
Add ¾ cup white vinegar
½ onion, grated, or chopped green onions
5 cans Del Monte tomato wedges, drained well. (If you cannot find wedges, I've used stewed tomatoes.)

Heat the oil and sugar until sugar melts. Pour the oil mixture over the tomatoes and onions in an airtight container. Refrigerate overnight. This will keep indefinitely. You can add up to 2 more cans of tomatoes to the original marinade. Drain well to serve.

Easy Asparagus Congealed Salad

1 (15-ounce) can cut asparagus
1 envelope unflavored gelatin
½ cup mayo
½ teaspoon Lawry's Seasoned Salt
¼ cup lemon juice
1 (8-ounce) carton whipping cream, or 1 (8-ounce) cottage cheese, whipped in a blender

Drain asparagus, pouring the liquid in a saucepan. Sprinkle gelatin over asparagus juice, and heat until gelatin dissolves. Cook 1 minute, stirring constantly. Let mixture cool in a large bowl. Combine mayo, lemon juice, and salt, and stir into gelatin mixture. Fold in whipping cream or cottage cheese. Add asparagus. Pour into mold(s), and chill until set. Makes 6–8 servings.

Reclaiming my youth with a latte spa day

Did you know that every time you throw your spent coffee grounds into the garbage, you're throwing away the key to youthfulness?

That statement was stamped in big red letters on a piece of junk mail urging me to subscribe to some off-the-wall medical newsletter. It was accompanied by a brochure pitching a home liposuction kit! Well, I never!

Oh, bunk, I thought. People will tell you anything to make a buck. Nevertheless, I began to ponder the possibilities. For years I've been throwing my spent coffee grounds on my azaleas, and they reward me every year with eye-popping blooms. Why NOT try it on my face?

I'm pretty much game for anything that promises that

youthful glow, and all those creams and goop can get pricey.

The very next day after brewing my coffee, I slathered the still-moist coffee grounds all over my face. I wandered out to my little courtyard to sip my coffee—while wearing my coffee. I stretched out on a lounge chair and listened to the sound of carpenter bees chomping merrily on my old garden shed.

Suddenly I heard the creak of the garden gate leading into my backyard. Oh double darn. Who in the world was coming back here at eight a.m. to interrupt my peaceful reverie . . . and discover my new skin care secret? I jumped out of my prone position and tried to dart behind the garden shed, when who should round the corner but the cute little meter reader?

The look on his face was priceless. "You're really getting into gardening," he commented, one eyebrow cocked an inch higher than the other.

"Oh, no. This isn't dirt," I assured him. "It's coffee grounds." (Like that should make a difference.)

"Okey dokey," he said. He walked a wide circle around me to look for the meter. He kept glancing in my direction as if he half expected me to pounce on him in a caffeine-induced rage.

But it was worth it all. After rinsing off the grounds, I could tell a difference—sort of. It seemed as if my skin WAS more supple, and instead of pale face I seemed a little "tan."

Here's how you do it. Spread the grounds of your morning coffee all over your face, adding a little Vaseline to help it adhere. Massage gently onto face, then allow to dry for 15–20 minutes. Rinse off with warm water. This will gently firm and tone your skin, minimizing pores and exfoliating so the fresh new skin underneath is revealed.

Before I schedule my next "latte spa day," I'm calling the electric department to make sure the meter reader isn't due to come by. Oh, and I did NOT order the home liposuction kit, tempted though I was.

The whole episode reminded me to go find Norma's Tipsy Mocha Punch recipe.

Tipsy Mocha Punch

2 cups hot-brewed, double-strength coffee
⅓ cup sugar
1 cup chocolate syrup
⅛ teaspoon cinnamon
1 gallon milk (2 percent is fine)
1 gallon vanilla ice cream
Libation of your choice–Norma thinks bourbon is best

Combine hot coffee, sugar, chocolate syrup, and cinnamon. Refrigerate until cool. Pour milk in a punch bowl and stir in coffee mixture. Add chunks of ice cream. Ladle into coffee or punch cups. If you're feeling frisky, you can add some bourbon.

Would you like flies with that?

I was strolling around my community farmer's market one sunny spring day. I languidly let my eyes feast on the beautiful produce and lovely loaves of artisanal breads while bobbing my head to the tunes of a bluegrass band. I'd intended to pick up some nice, juicy Early Girl tomatoes, maybe a just-picked head of lettuce, and some sourdough bread on which to build the perfect BLT for lunch.

Caught up in the moment and on the advice of well-meaning foodie friends, I ended up purchasing some completely foreign vegetables I never planned to consume in this lifetime. Before I knew what was happening, a bunch of kale and some bok choy found their way into my bag. I must admit it gave me a rush; I was feeling all worldly and sophisticated.

I've known about kale for many years but never knew it was edible. I thought it was just to decorate the plate (kind of like beets).

As instructed by my "advisors," I went home and cooked the kale up in a skillet with some olive oil and Parmesan cheese—I mean, what's not good with olive oil and Parmesan cheese? I settled down to what I was told would be the healthiest lunch on the planet. Maybe so—if you can get it down. The kale just got larger the more I chewed, and I had to spit it out when it threatened to choke me to death. I'd sooner eat grass clippings and shredded magnolia leaves. It was horrible!

Now I hear that the food Nazis are suggesting we give up meat and begin eating insects (that's BUGS, folks). They are plentiful and supposedly packed with protein and healthy fats.

I don't care if they're packed with 20-carat diamonds. They will never be served on my table. I am completely unsettled by the thought of eating the same creatures that make me squeal and dash for the nearest shoe. Like most Americans, I was raised to deplore most creepy-crawlies in any form. Yet insects are treated as delicacies in places like Colombia, where I'm told ant larvae are served in theaters like popcorn, and in Mexico, where street vendors sell roasted grasshoppers seasoned with chili and lime.

Margaret Ann recently celebrated her fiftieth wedding anniversary with a trip to Belize. She swears she ate termites while taking a nature walk in the rain forest. They were LIVE termites, and I'm sure they tickled going down.

Yes, believe it or not, insects may be a viable solution to the world's inevitable food shortage, but I hope not in my lifetime. Population observers generally agree the Earth will be home to roughly nine billion people by 2050, and the food police are madly searching for answers as to how to feed our next great baby boom.

Eating bugs would certainly resolve my weight issues, because I'd rather starve than chow down on a plate of barbecued locust. On the other hand, when you think about it, bugs aren't all that different from crawfish, which are even called mudbugs by my Louisiana buddies.

Eating bugs would also help alleviate the need for pest control. Instead of the bugs eating us, we could begin eating them first. We could become hunters and gatherers every evening when the moths begin fluttering around the front porch light. I'll opt for some of my low-calorie peanut butter cups (yes, you read that right, the ultimate oxymoron). But hold the flies.

Dieter's Peanut Butter Cups

8 ounces Cool Whip
½ cup crunchy peanut butter
Reese's Shell Topping Peanut Butter Sauce

Line small muffin pans with paper liners. Mix Cool Whip and peanut butter until well-incorporated. Spoon into lined muffin pan. Top with a swirl of Reese's sauce. Freeze 6–8 hours. Once solid, you can place in a freezer bag and keep for those times when you just gotta have a Reese's.

Dancing when no one is looking

Sometimes it feels as if there are two people living in my body. They are completely different personalities, each fighting for control. I don't think they like each other very much.

One is a sweet gentle creature who likes to lounge in the world's most comfortable recliner with a good murder mystery and a bag of Reese's Peanut Butter Cups. The other is a restless, frustrated woman who starts new projects weekly, knowing full well she will never finish any of them. She rearranges the furniture in her house at least once a month and recently swapped out the dining room for the living room. Now no one knows where to go when she says "Dinner is served."

With my new expanded living room, I have room for an activity both ladies in my body can enjoy (dancing) but only when the curtains are drawn and no one is watching. Oh, I also sing when no one can hear. Not only is it fun and great exercise, I think those squirrels living in my attic have moved on. They probably got tired of hearing all the stomping around to the tune of "Brick House," which rattles the windows.

I began my dancing career this spring while looking around for a new fitness program that doesn't involve getting down on the floor or sweating in the summer heat. I read a report in the *New England Journal of Medicine* that showed a lower risk for dementia among people over sixty-five who regularly danced during their leisure time. But what was so surprising about the report is that other types of physical exercise didn't affect the dementia risk—dancing was the only physical activity that made a difference. Baby, I'm in!

It doesn't matter what type of dance you choose. Mine is "freestyle," which incorporates a bit of a high kickin' Irish jig, the tango, the bebop, and watusi. It doesn't really matter so long as your body moves constantly and energetically so that you're elevating your heart rate and burning calories. I draw the line at breakdancing because I would probably break something, including a lamp or body part.

By all means, turn the music up to the max and sing along, but you might want to wait until your closest neighbors have gone to work. I may even install a pole and a disco ball so I can ramp up my routine even more.

Richard Powers, a dance professor at Stanford University, explains that freestyle dance actually requires more brain-power than choreographed routines. You make rapid decisions about how you move, rather than following a predetermined set of steps. Supposedly this helps reduce the risk of dementia more than any other physical activity.

Freestyle dancing is easy to do anytime, anywhere; you don't need a dance floor, a partner, or a wide open space. You can dance standing in front of your desk, or on top of your desk for that matter. You can dance around your kitchen as you prepare dinner. My favorite kitchen routine is called slap dancing. You simply move your feet around while slapping together a tomato sandwich.

I'll never be on *Dancing with the Stars*, but I have worked up a couple of routines I can perform during commercial breaks. There's the Omaha Traveler, where I hop around while swinging an imaginary baseball bat. I invented the dance while watching the Super Regional NCAA baseball games one year.

For even more fun, dance in front of a mirror (if you can stand to look). I promise you a good laugh, and a better mood will follow you wherever you go for the rest of the day. Best of all, you will burn oodles of calories and you can whip up something good and eat it guilt-free . . . like my Aunt Emma's mayo-less pimento cheese. This is fabulous, folks, and perfect for a picnic because it doesn't contain mayonnaise.

Aunt Emma's Pimento Cheese, Hold the Mayo

This freezes beautifully, and I take a tub of it to all Mississippi State baseball games. As Rachael Ray says, "Yummo!!!"

1 pound grated Velveeta (if you freeze it a few minutes it's easier to grate)
10 ounces sharp Cheddar cheese, grated (she swears by Cracker Barrel)
½ pound Mexican Velveeta, grated
2 (4-ounce) jars chopped pimentos and juice
3 tablespoons white vinegar
Spicy brown mustard, about half a bottle
2 tablespoons sugar

Mix all ingredients until creamy and fully incorporated.

I made appetizers the other day spreading this pimento cheese on miniature rye bread and then placing it under the broiler till browned.

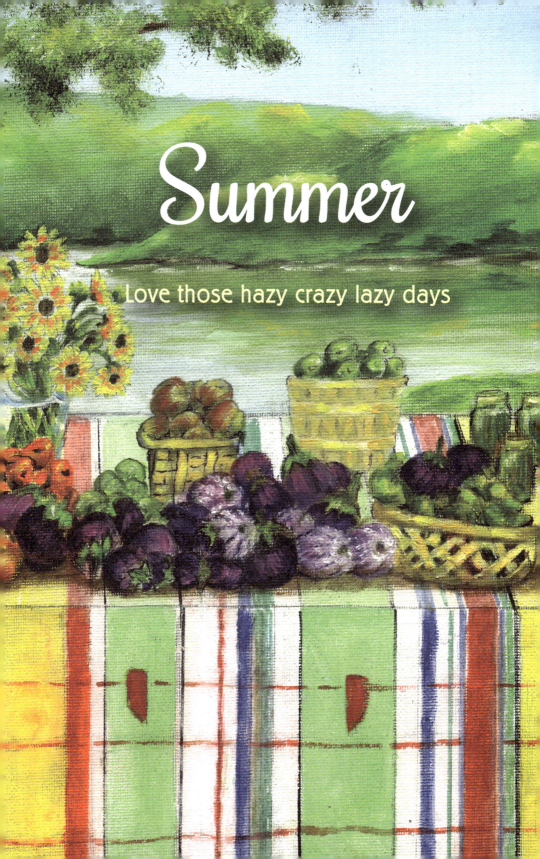

Summer

Love those hazy crazy lazy days

Life's sweeter in a small town

Comedians joke about them, big-city folks cast aspersions on them, and big business pretends they don't exist.

Of course, I'm talking about small towns—the place where you know all your neighbors and a trip to the Piggly Wiggly is the social event of the week.

When I lived in New Orleans, I could sneak into Target without makeup or even matching shoes, confident I wouldn't meet a soul I knew. Now I can't get out of Kroger without running into my dentist, my CPA, my hairdresser, and a third cousin. Perfect strangers become fast friends as we wait in the checkout line.

When I dashed to the store last week without makeup, three people expressed concern that I was ill. One even brought me some chicken soup later in the day. What a testament to the power of makeup!

Take my advice, you'd better get dressed to the nines to go steppin' out in my town, even if going out is only to pay your electric bill. And, never, ever plan to be in a hurry.

There's no such thing as dashing into the store for a quick loaf of bread. You'll run into at least four or five people you know. There will be grandbaby photos to oooh and aaah over. And I never leave the store without a good recipe or two.

While waiting at the checkout counter, my favorite thing to ask is "Excuse me, ma'am. What are you going to do with those Butterfingers?" (Or whatever they're buying that I'm not.) Okay, so I'm nosy, but I either find out that there's a great sale on candy bars . . . or she will write down the recipe for some family favorite on the back of her grocery list. Today I obtained a recipe for Butterfinger Pie, which must be the easiest confection ever devised for harried housewives.

Mary Jo Hill's Lightning Quick Butterfinger Pie

1 (9-inch) pie crust, baked and cooled
10 fun-size or 2 king-size Butterfinger bars
1 small tub Cool Whip

Crush Butterfingers while still in their wrappers (this is good for releasing tension). Unwrap and crush any remaining large pieces. Mix with Cool Whip and pour into pie crust. Freeze and keep frozen until ready to serve.

When I selected the community in which to retire, I hit the jackpot. Starkville, Mississippi, is still small enough to qualify for the small town moniker, yet it bumps smack dab into a major university which adds energy and nightly opportunities for concerts, plays, and sporting events.

Thank goodness I didn't pick some huge honking metropolis. I would have been gobbled up and spit out during the first few weeks. Here, I have more activities than I can pencil in, and doing a leisurely lunch is my favorite pastime.

Small town. The designation evokes fond memories of the small community where I grew up as well as the one I adopted when I felt the need to slow down and enjoy life. Both offer an intimate sense of community, leafy serenity, and freedom from the cold, grimy canyons of the big city.

Linda's Asparagus Sandwiches

This recipe took my small town by storm back in the 70s. I think the late Mrs. Nina Clark originated it.

2 hard boiled eggs, grated
1 can asparagus tips, drained
3 ounces cream cheese
Lawry's seasoned salt (Linda said to guess at how much)
Thin sliced white bread, crusts trimmed
Melted butter
Parmesan cheese

Grate eggs and cream together with cream cheese, asparagus, and seasoned salt. Spread mixture on a slice of bread and top with a second slice. Cut in quarters and dip in melted butter. (At this stage they may be frozen.) When ready to serve, sprinkle liberally with Parmesan cheese and broil on both sides. Delicious.

Closing down the kitchen for summer

Did you know that there are some places in the world where the kitchen has become optional? People of the younger generation are actually building homes without kitchens, opting for a mere corner for the latte maker and microwave.

I think this trend is happening mostly in New York and other highly populated areas where space is limited and folks under the age of fifty never learned to cook and they aren't interested in learning.

Until about two weeks ago I was cooking ninety percent of my meals at home and making a mess reminiscent of the eruption of Mount Vesuvius every day of my life. (That's the volcano that buried Pompeii, and I was working on a similar fate.)

The endless repetitiveness of it all—cooking and cleaning up, cooking and cleaning up—was beginning to get me down. Cooking and cleaning are boring, lonely activities, and they never seem to end. But I guess I said that already.

I decided to liberate myself from this act of slavery and close down my kitchen for the rest of the summer. I'll do something else in there . . . maybe incubate dinosaur eggs or fire the odd piece of pottery. Freed from kitchen duty, I feel like a new woman. There's no grocery shopping and no dishwasher to clean out. This is the most brilliant idea I've ever had!

What about eating, you may ask? No problem. I just ditch the china and silverware and eat from Styrofoam containers with plastic forks and dine on food someone else cooked.

While researching a magazine article on that seductive genre of cuisine known as the "Blue Plate Special," I was forced to test the "meat and three" options in no less than fourteen local restaurants. I lined up with all the other comfort-food junkies and chowed down on meatloaf, mac 'n cheese, turnip greens, fried green tomatoes, and mashed potatoes and gravy.

I started out wearing my skinny jeans and concluded the experiment wearing a 1980s industrial-sized muumuu. I did all this in a two-week period when my washing machine went on the blink and shrank my jeans by at least two sizes. (That's my story and I'm sticking to it.)

Realizing I couldn't continue on that path to obesity, I now allow myself one Blue Plate per day, purchased at eleven a.m. while the selections are freshest. I go home, carefully halve the portions, and dump them into another container to save for dinner. Since most area blue plates average about $7 (including drink), I figure I will spend around $200 a month, which is less than I was spending on groceries when I was doing all the shopping, hard labor, and clean up. My water and power bills should plummet, too.

This is a win/win situation for me. When fall returns and temperatures moderate, I'll probably reopen the kitchen and slog around, making my usual messes. Till then, I'm on summer vacation and enjoying the extra time I get to read, relax, and think. I wear myself out thinking sometimes. But I have no menu to plan or grocery list to buy. I'm just a free-wheeling, happy-go-lucky, lazy girl, waiting for the line to form at the nearest diner. Keep your kitchen clean and eat out often this summer. Or try this refreshing tuna salad idea when the girls come over. The recipe, bequeathed to me by my Mama M, takes the humble can of tuna to a whole new level . . . and no oven is required.

Very Sophisticated Tuna Salad

2 cans white Albacore tuna, drained
1 package frozen green peas (cooked and cooled)
¾ cup mayonnaise
2 tablespoons lemon juice
¼ teaspoon garlic salt or powder
½ teaspoon curry powder
2 tablespoons soy sauce
1 small jar cocktail onions (about ¾ cup)
½ cup sliced almonds or chopped pecans
1 can chow mein noodles

The day before you plan to serve, mix all ingredients, except nuts and noodles. Refrigerate. Add nuts and noodles just before serving. Mama M always served these with fresh asparagus, Sun Chips, and plenty of sweet iced tea.

Nothing like true love and homegrown tomatuhs

There are a few things in life that are worth the effort required for the benefits derived—true love and homegrown tomatoes are the first two that come to mind.

Actually I borrowed that philosophy from a country singer. On Saturday, I felt the urge to hit the open road for an adventure and a trip to my old hometown—Madison, Mississippi. Well, let me tell you one thing. It's not the sleepy little town I left 15 years ago. I could hardly find it. It's run smack dab into the City of Jackson, and I got hopelessly lost trying to find my old home.

I timed my trip perfectly to accompany "The Garden Mama" (our regional garden authority) from start to finish on the Super Talk Mississippi network. Nellie Neal has been doing a Saturday morning radio show as long as I can remember, but I never get to hear it from start to finish. I catch a snippet here and there as I perform my Saturday morning chores.

Her bumper music was playing just as I cranked the car, and she was putting the show to bed two hours later as I pulled into Madison. But I enjoyed myself immensely as I drove along dusty Mississippi roads and heard a variety of garden problems solved. (I don't like driving the sterile four lanes, opting instead for the back roads which took me up Highway 16 to Canton and beyond.)

The high point of the show for me was the annual playing of Guy Clark's country music song "Homegrown Tomatoes." It's a catchy little ditty that suggests nothing but homegrown tomatoes can rival true love.

Thankfully the country crooner was wrong. You CAN buy homegrown tomatuhs if you know where to look or make friends with a farmer. My taste buds are gearing up for my two most favorite foods: a sliced homegrown tomatuh and homemade pimento cheese . . . slathered on a piece of plain white bread. Oh, and hold the sprouts and seven grains. This has got to be white bread which you can still buy for less than a dollar a loaf.

Of course, like any self-respecting redneck, I love eating a tomatuh sandwich standing over the kitchen sink and letting the juice run down my arm and down the drain. When tomatoes are at their peak, my friends Caroline Atkins and Olivia Portera like to pick a few for their special versions of fresh tomato pie. Oooh-wee. As we say in Mississippi, it's "gone" be good!

Caroline Harrell Atkins' Fresh Tomato Pie

1 (9-inch) pie shell
3–4 large homegrown tomatoes
1 cup mayonnaise–I favor Blue Plate
2 cups shredded Cheddar cheese
3–4 slices bacon

Bake pie shell at 350° until brown. Slice tomatoes, and arrange in pie crust. Salt and pepper to taste. Mix mayo and cheese together, and spread on tomatoes. Return to oven and bake until cheese melts (about 25–30 minutes). While pie is in oven, cook bacon in microwave until crisp. Crumble bacon and sprinkle on top of pie during the last five minutes of baking. Let pie cool 10–15 minutes before cutting (if you can stand it).

Sally's Tomato Pie
From the recipe file of Olivia Portera

2 or 3 Vidalia onions
3–4 large homegrown tomatoes
Unbaked pie shell (I use Pillsbury in a roll)
4 very ripe tomatoes
1 (16-ounce) package grated four-cheese blend

Slice onions (thick slices) and sauté in butter with a little fresh basil. Slice tomatoes and toss with a little flour and salt and pepper. In pie shell, layer tomatoes, onions, and cheese; repeat, ending with cheese. Bake at 350° on bottom shelf of oven for 30–40 minutes. Remove from oven and let sit for 10 minutes.

Jogging in a bottle beats a run in the heat, sort of

Can you handle one more miracle cure for everything from obesity to arthritis?

Hold on. Don't shut the book until you hear me out. I know I've raised hopes in the past only to have them dashed by worthless solutions (i.e. the ear stapling hoax for weight loss). In case you're wondering, I gained three pounds after having my ear stapled, and it set me back $50! Gullibility has always been one of my strong suits.

But this latest "miracle cure" could provide relief from a whole range of thorny problems associated with aging, so listen up.

I recently had the great pleasure of reconnecting with a high school friend who has moved to my community. She looks great and spends her free time cycling and running up and down the bleachers at the local high school to stay in shape. My exercise routine involves pushing a grocery cart around the supermarket and lumbering up and down the steps at the First Presbyterian Church once a week.

As Marie described her regimen, she casually mentioned that she uses a concoction called "Jogging in a Bottle" to reduce joint pain and maintain weight loss. Intrigued, I begged for more information.

Apparently, someone was marketing the "happy juice" in the Jackson area, but she managed to figure out the formula. In a nutshell, it was a mixture of grape juice, apple juice, and apple cider vinegar. You take a jigger-full several times a day and wait for the aches, pains, and appetite to subside.

"I began taking it for joint pain, but I quit smoking instead," Marie declared (like there was some connection). Confused, I was having a hard time following her train of thought, but mentally I was already plotting an escape to get to the store to pick up the ingredients. I was chug-a-lugging the tart cocktail by bedtime . . . and would compare it to licking the port-o-potty at Woodstock.

Marie couldn't believe I'd never heard of this miracle cure, because jogging in a bottle was apparently making the rounds about the time I was getting my ears stapled. The juice was so named because supposedly you could drink it *in place of* jogging. (How far, I'm not sure—maybe only to the kitchen sink to spit it out.)

I suddenly remembered Daddy telling me that his mother drank a vinegar mixture every day of her life, and she lived to be ninety-eight years old. She wasn't overweight, either, but she did dip snuff.

If an apple a day keeps the doctor away, doesn't it seem logical that apple cider vinegar might be just as effective?

Jogging in a Bottle
(secret recipe)

2 tablespoons apple cider vinegar (must contain the "mother"
  —I use Bragg's, which is available at most Kroger stores)
½ cup grape juice
¼ cup apple cider
1 tablespoon honey or maple syrup

Mix together and chug.

Oh, what the heck, just turn up the bottle of vinegar and take a healthy nip to save on calories from the juice and honey. It is also supposed to whiten your teeth (if it doesn't eat off the enamel) and regulate blood sugar. It works for Marie.

Tales of a former food snob

Once upon a time I fancied myself a gourmet cook. I put paper booties on my standing rib roasts and added white truffle oil to my grits. I stuffed every vegetable I could find, thinking it couldn't possibly taste good on its own.

Mine was a simple case of "cooking to impress" to cover my inherent inadequacies in the kitchen. The sad truth is, my Southern mother never taught me to cook because I made such a mess in the kitchen. Still do.

Consequently, I disguised my disability regarding the basics of country cooking and became a self-proclaimed food snob. I took a course in French cuisine and served highbrow fare like Boeuf Bourguignon and Coq au Vin. Looking back, those things were never well-received at my Super Bowl parties, even when I did them well.

I considered butterbeans and cornbread beneath me. I would practice saying "Care for a canapé?" and served dinner (never supper) with little finger bowls, until a day when one of my cowboy boot-wearing guests blurted out "What the heck are these for?"

I lifted one eyebrow, a talent I learned as a coed at Ole Miss. You have probably noticed how it's used mostly by pretentious people. As I attempted to explain the function of a finger bowl, I burst out laughing. It dawned on me how ridiculous I looked wearing my black cocktail dress while serving boiled crawfish on my perfectly-appointed table with its starched white linens and polished silver.

Then Mr. Finger Bowl Man got up, went to the kitchen, and brought back a roll of paper towels and a stack of old newspapers.

We removed the crystal and linens, kicked off our shoes, and ate the rest of the meal with our fingers. Eating was fun again. I felt as if I was finally home after wandering in the wilderness of haute cuisine with names I couldn't pronounce, much less prepare.

Clearly, I had been led down the garden path of hoity-toity food—nice to look at, but scoring few points in my native South. I'm learning to cook all over again, and I've developed an obsession with Southern culture and the simple, humble food I grew up with.

Hold the designer oils and food wardrobe and bring on the grits and greens. I've rediscovered the joys of sweet corn straight from the field and a pot of sweet potatoes cooked for hours with real butter and sugar (the nectar of the gods). And give me a plate of fried green tomatoes with maybe a little ranch dressing on the side. (My homegrown vine has yet to produce a red tomato because I am compelled to fry 'em up green.)

Replicating the food my grandmother cooked is my new passion. I'm collecting recipes for traditional Southern fare like pimento cheese and deviled eggs. I'm dreaming of a pot of black-eyed peas—bathed in pot likker and cooked until almost unrecognizable.

Before leaving the market, I picked up some fresh squash for Margaret Ann's squash boats.

Margaret Ann's tip of the day:

Margaret Ann's mother also made stuffed tomatoes similar to the stuffed squash. She would cut the top slightly off the tomato, take a spoon, and dig out all the inside pulp, being careful not to break through the skin and reserving the pulp for another use. Drain hollowed out tomatoes upside down on a paper towel before stuffing. Add poultry seasoning to the stuffing to taste (see recipe on next page). Margaret Ann's mother always used real cornbread. Sometimes Margaret Ann "cheats" and uses the bought cornbread stuffing.

Tibbee Creek Squash Boats

Tibbee Creek is a major landmark in the area where Margaret Ann and I grew up. A squash boat would be about the largest vessel to navigate its waters.

1 nice yellow squash per person (let's say 6–8)
½ medium onion, diced
½ bell pepper, seeded and diced
4 tablespoons real butter
½ box cornbread stuffing
Chicken broth
2 dashes Worcestershire sauce
Dash white pepper
Pinch of cayenne pepper
Olive oil cooking spray
Crushed potato chips

Cut squash in half lengthwise, and cook in salted water with onion and bell pepper until tender, drain. With a spoon or melon baller, scoop out squash pulp. Spray hollowed out squash boats with olive oil inside and out.

Combine squash pulp, stuffing, butter, and enough chicken broth to moisten. Add Worcestershire sauce, white pepper, and a pinch of cayenne. Spoon stuffing inside each boat, and arrange in 9x13-inch glass dish. Add a little chicken broth, and cover with foil. Bake at 275° until boats are soft to the touch. Sprinkle tops with crushed potato chips.

Down on the funny farm

I missed out on the hippie movement of the 1970s because I thought I wanted to be a banker. The banking environment wasn't receptive to T-shirts and earth shoes, so I squeezed myself into a navy blue suit and unbearably high heels and called myself a banker. I never did figure out how to compute a percentage.

That career was short-lived, so I moved on to even more unsuitable vocations—all the while longing to be in the great outdoors digging in the dirt. The greatest gift a parent can give a child is to advise him (or her) to figure out what he likes to do . . . then pursue a career in that area. Those lucky children will never have to work a day in their lives!

Fast forward about four decades. I've decided to give in to my natural urges to grow and nurture things. One big problem: I have a garden the size of a postage stamp. It's surrounded on all four sides by towering oak trees which cast deep shadows on the property. I can't grow monkey grass, much less a cucumber.

Thankfully, a friend with a huge backyard offered the space to do with as I please, although he did draw the line on my plans for a goat and a few chickens. He provides the land and the water, I contribute the plants and supplies, and my son Braddock tends the whole thing.

We had a major hurdle to overcome. We know zilch about urban farming. When the three of us get together to do our "gardening," I'm reminded of The Three Stooges. We bump into each other and get tangled up in the hoses. On day two, we discovered most of the tender sprouts had been attacked by slugs. We poured beer into bowls and placed them around the garden, a new twist on the term "beer garden." The slugs hop in, slurp up the beer, and can't get out. At least they die happy.

We had dreams of a bumper crop of exotic vegetables. We planted eighteen heirloom tomatoes with strange names like Baltic Stupice, Bloody Bath, Caspian Pink, and Black Krim. We also planted sugar snap peas and an assortment of squashes and peppers. My new variety of Drunken Woman Frizzy-Headed Lettuce is already being harvested, but it's a tad bitter.

We also planted some Trinidad Scorpion Peppers. This is the hottest pepper known to man—it scores a million units on the Scoville scale. I don't know what we will do with them . . . make pepper spray, perhaps?

I'm thinking of reserving a space at the Community Market to sell what we can't consume. There's a limit to how many BLTs one can eat on a hot summer day. I also plan to make my own tomato sauce and can it up in Ball jars. Move over, Paul

Newman, I'm giving you a run for your money.

I figure I've spent around $400 in setting up this garden. Crazy? Yes. We could have purchased tomatoes for the next three years for less than that. But, hey, it's a hobby. Golfers, who spend a fortune on green fees and hi-tech metal clubs may forever remain weekend duffers. Fishermen who spend thousands on boats and lures may never bring home anything larger than a minnow.

If we get only a dozen tomatoes, it will be okay. You can bury a lot of troubles digging in the dirt. It occurs to me that urban farmers are the ultimate study in hopeful people. We do all this work without any idea what we are doing, yet hold out hope that something will grow and produce.

I've learned one lesson. Don't wear perfume to the garden unless you want to be pollinated by a herd of bees. And for those days when your garden is spitting out eggplant and squashes like watermelon seeds, try this recipe.

Oven-Fried Eggplant
(no oil needed)

½ cup fine bread crumbs (Panko crumbs work nicely, too)
½ cup Parmesan cheese
¼ teaspoon salt
¼ teaspoon pepper
1 eggplant
⅓ cup light mayonnaise
Fresh basil, chopped

Combine bread crumbs, Parmesan cheese, and salt and pepper. Peal eggplant (you don't have to, but I find the peel distasteful), and cut into ¼-inch slices. Spread both sides with a thin coat of mayonnaise. Dredge in crumb mixture. Place on lightly-greased baking sheet. Bake at 400° for 10–12 minutes. Turn over about halfway through cooking. Garnish with fresh chopped basil.

Note: Although the recipe doesn't call for it, I usually sprinkle the eggplant slices liberally with salt and let them sit for about half an hour to draw out any bitterness. Just wash off salt and dry well before proceeding.

Confused by the new dietary rules

I stay in a constant state of confusion. Turn on the television set or open a newspaper and there it is . . . the latest "Nutrition Study of the Week." It contradicts last week's "Nutrition Study of the Week."

Eggs are bad, then eggs are okay. Butter is better than margarine, and the sun peeks from behind the clouds. Caffeine is identified as a killer, and the sun disappears. We begin drinking caffeine-free coffee, and we nod off while operating machinery.

Just when you think you have gotten to the bottom of the whole vexing question of food and health, you get blown away by the tailwinds of the latest study which flies in the face of traditional thinking. I've probably taken a thousand bottles of calcium supplements in my lifetime, only to learn they may cause heart disease. So I wander around like Fred Sanford expecting "the big one" any minute now: "Hold on Elizabeth, I'm coming."

And diet? Back in the 60s, they told us low-fat was the way to go. We began counting calories, eating low-fat products, and scowling a lot. Now I read that as a nation, we have only gotten fatter—obese even. One study reports that during that same period, women's waist sizes grew by six inches (from 28 to 34). I wonder who did that study, and where were the men? Why do they get off so easy?

Has anyone thought of doing a study of people who do the studies? I have this vision of a room full of evil people armed with clipboards trying to decide which substance will be on their hit list next week. Things like caffeine and sugar are their favorite targets—probably because people actually like them.

Why don't they target icky things like Brussels sprouts or English peas? If you like these two vegetables, I'm sorry. To me, they taste the way dirty socks smell.

I'm still angry about the way chocolate was treated back during my adolescence. Studies said it caused acne, so it was banned from my house. I saved up my meager allowance and sneaked Hershey Bars at the movie theater. Frankly, I didn't have any more blemishes than anyone else.

Today, studies show that chocolate is the elixir of life and wonderful for our health. We should have some every day. I wouldn't be surprised if a study comes along touting nicotine and DDT as desirable substances, and we all can begin dipping snuff and buying poison on the black market.

Here's my new rule of thumb: Don't ingest anything your

great grandmother wouldn't recognize. That would include Fiddle Faddle, Go-Gurt, and any cheese spray in a can.

Be suspicious of any food you see advertised on television. Chances are it started out as a whole food of some sort, then became altered by ingredients you can't identify, much less spell. Bet you haven't seen any ads for spinach or onions lately, have you?

If it came from a plant, eat it. If it was MADE in a plant, don't. That's the rule (unless it's peanut butter, which is exempt from all rules). That reminds me, you may want to try one of my all-time favorites: my Aunt Emma's Peanut Butter Pie.

Make It in Your Sleep Peanut Butter Pie

1 cup peanut butter, creamy or chunky (your choice, but I like crunchy)
1 cup confectioner's sugar
8 ounces Cool Whip
4 ounces cream cheese, softened
1 (9-inch) graham cracker pie shell

Mix first 4 ingredients together and pour into pie shell. Freeze until 30 minutes before serving.

Sometimes Aunt Emma puts the filling into a chocolate graham pie shell and drizzles the top with Hershey's syrup, especially for Easter Dinner. I've been known to eat half a pie after everyone has gone home.

faking a clean house

I'm a notorious serial cleaner when it comes to housekeeping. On average I clean about as often as the full moon appears, but over the years I've figured out how to fake it with a moment's notice when necessary.

Turns out, clean isn't all that hard to fake. Here's how you can pull it off in a few easy steps.

So, you're lolling about in your PJs, anticipating a lazy day. The phone rings and it's your college roommate, whom you haven't seen in twenty-five years. She's passing through town and wants to stop by and say hello. (Translation: she always suspected you were a bit of a slob, and she wants to confirm it.)

The **first step** is to give her the sketchiest directions imaginable. Make sure she must stop for additional directions at least twice. This will give you fifteen minutes to clean house and fifteen minutes to put on your game face (the one you wear to public events).

The **second step** is to run around the kitchen in a circle waving your arms for thirty seconds. This will release all tension and calm you down.

Step three: Grab a big basket roughly the size of your oven. Fill it with every piece of clutter in the living area. In go magazines, your running shoes, umbrella, dirty dishes . . . everything. Make doubly sure you scoop up all your "old-lady" stuff (tissues, nasal spray, prescription drugs) and stuff them into the box.

Now, cram the box into the oven. Just don't forget it, or you will have the fire department as your next house guest.

I try to reserve one side of my sofa cushions to be shown to guests. Quickly flip over the cushions to reveal good-as-new fabric. When she leaves, you can flip back to "slob" side. If, like me, you've forgotten to do the "company flip," just drape a colorful throw over the bad spots. Strategically placed, throw pillows can also camouflage many past sins.

Step four: Make up the bed (with the dog still in it if necessary). Grab a second box and swipe everything off your bedside table and dresser. Stow it in your closet.

While you're in there, pull out your one outfit that makes you look thin. Put on lipstick and fluff your hair with some baby powder. Voila, instant big hair. The baby powder acts as a dry shampoo.

Step five: Find the strongest-smelling cleaner under your sink, wipe off the counter tops, and pour some down the drain. (You might want to take a nip while you're at it.)

Take the rest of the house and shove it in the guest room. Dash back to the kitchen table and sit casually as if you've been chatting on the phone. If your calculations are correct, she will be coming up the drive about now.

"Oh, look who's here! Come on in, I've just been sitting here reading the paper!"

To impress your old friend even more, take a page from the playbook of my late friend Frances McReynolds on stress-free entertaining.

No-Brainer Appetizer BLTs

6–8 slices of white bread (or more depending on how many you plan to serve and how hungry you are.)

Mayonnaise (I like Duke's; Margaret Ann likes Hellmann's)

Ripe, firm tomatoes, sliced roughly the same diameter as your bread rounds

Italian seasoning to taste

Cracked black pepper and kosher salt, to taste

5–6 slices bacon

6–8 teaspoons Parmesan cheese

Cut bread into rounds with a scalloped cookie cutter (if you can find one). Spread each round with mayonnaise, and top with a tomato slice. Sprinkle with Italian seasoning, salt, and pepper. Top with crumbled bacon and a teaspoon of Parmesan cheese. Bake at 375° until bread is crisp and cheese is bubbly. Yummo!

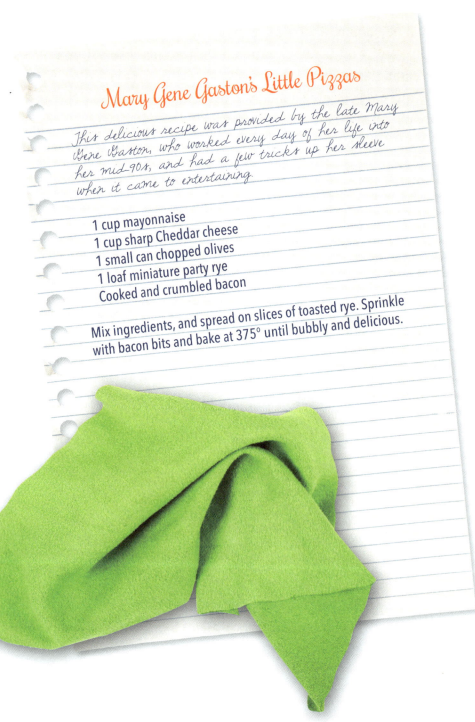

Mary Gene Gaston's Little Pizzas

This delicious recipe was provided by the late Mary Gene Gaston, who worked every day of her life into her mid-90s, and had a few tricks up her sleeve when it came to entertaining.

1 cup mayonnaise
1 cup sharp Cheddar cheese
1 small can chopped olives
1 loaf miniature party rye
Cooked and crumbled bacon

Mix ingredients, and spread on slices of toasted rye. Sprinkle with bacon bits and bake at 375° until bubbly and delicious.

The health benefits of creative loafing

I was all set to do a column on quantum physics or the molecular structure of hair color, but something more important came up which should have a greater impact on civilization.

So I redirected my thoughts and research into "the virtues of loafing." I'm not talking about professional relaxation like yoga, meditation, or anything remotely complicated. I'm talking about putting your feet up, placing your worries on hold, and chilling out for a couple of hours. A little dozing doesn't hurt. The noise and confusion of your everyday world are temporarily blocked, and you are likely to hear the tiny voice in your soul (which you thought had moved to Hawaii).

To get started, you need special attire to loaf properly—the older and baggier the better. Who doesn't come home from some fancy affair, only to begin peeling off the scratchy, too-tight outfit before you're fully out of the car?

I have a drawer full of my loafing gear, which includes soft, oft-washed sweats, a furry bathrobe that makes me look like a stuffed polar bear, and my house shoes (in a camouflage print which I found at Fred's for five dollars. Best five bucks I ever spent). Best of all, they are shaped like loafers, which I deemed perfect for a day of loafing.

I've been caught wearing them to the supermarket, and I'm always prepared to feign shock. "Oh, I'm mortified!" I exclaim as I point down to my house shoes. "I flat forgot to change into my stilettos!" No one is fooled.

If you're feeling especially uptight and stressed, a whole afternoon of loafing can recharge your batteries. It doesn't have to be passive. Aggressive loafing can include beating your weeds with a baseball bat, chasing down drivers with mind-numbing boom boxes to get their tag numbers, and throwing burgers on the grill.

I wonder if that well-meaning Benjamin Franklin knew how much misery he would cause the world when—back in 1757 and high on puritanical zeal—he declared, "Early to bed and early to rise makes a man healthy, wealthy and wise." I'm here to tell you: IT'S JUST NOT SO. I follow his advice every day and I'm not all that healthy, far from wealthy, and my wisdom comes from the realization that I really know nothing at all.

One of the things I dislike about the time change is that my nine o'clock bedtime will soon coincide with the setting sun, thereby extending the time I feel compelled to be out and about, doing whatever society expects of a social butterfly whose wings are a bit faded and tattered.

In the winter, darkness falls around five p.m., and I can knock off and settle in for some creative loafing without guilt. A good loaf for me is always accompanied by a murder mystery and a big bowl of M&Ms. But, hey, I eat only the brightly-colored greens, reds, and yellows because they are supposed to be heart healthy.

How about an easy recipe for chocolate chip cookies to accompany your loaf? You can even substitute those healthful M&Ms if you like.

Mary Jo's No-Hassle Chocolate Chip Cookies

1 box yellow cake mix
1 cup sugar
1 cup oil
2 eggs
1 tablespoon vanilla
2 cups quick-cooking oats
½ –1 (12-ounce) package chocolate chips
1–2 cups chopped pecans

Combine all ingredients, adding pecans last until mixture is very stiff. Drop by tablespoonfuls into greased cookie sheet. Bake 17 minutes in 350° oven.

Dealing with an empty seat at my dinner table

My golden retriever Cajun didn't actually sit at my dining room table to eat her meals, but then neither do I. At meal times she assumed her favorite crouch beside the chair where I read, nap, write emails, watch television. And often curse politicians.

Cleaning up after me seemed to be her life's mission. This gentle yet nimble golden retriever with the perpetual smile (and a tail that could beat perfect time to the Mississippi State fight song) could catch a wayward crumb in midair without any warning.

Her crowning achievement was keeping my kitchen floors spotless. The only thing she refused to lap up with gusto was the Civil War hardtack I once attempted to make for a program at the public library. I think she confused it with clay pot shards.

Cajun knew all my secrets and kept her sense of humor with an impish, yet perceptive grin that assured me that my foibles were safe with her. She watched with amusement as I stashed my mail and other papers in the oven when friends dropped by unannounced. Then, I swear she stifled a giggle hours later when I preheated the oven for a Lean Cuisine and baked my mail to a golden brown.

She lived for those times when I lapsed into a chocolate binge with a carton of Moose Tracks. I would pick out all the chocolate tidbits, then save a few calories by placing the melting ice cream container on the floor for her to lap up. Of course, that was before I learned sweets weren't good for those of the canine persuasion (although she most definitely was NOT just a dog). In spite of her human diet, she still lived to the ripe old age of 94 . . . in doggy years.

On the morning she died she was still chasing her old nemesis—the hated red squirrel that had tormented her for almost four years. Old age and painful joints kept Cajun from being a real threat to "Ole Red," but she always made the effort anyway, especially if someone was watching.

At eight a.m. on Sunday, Cajun went to the great doggy heaven in the sky, where I hope no squirrels are allowed. She died while my son Braddock and I sat beside her assuring her everything was going to be okay.

After she took her last breath, we took her to B's hunting camp near the Noxubee Refuge where she loved to swim with the catfish. We buried her underneath the oaks overlooking the lake. I fashioned a headstone from one of my treasured Chicago bricks (salvaged from the old Howard Furniture

Company when it was demolished).

I suppose Rebel, my fearless little Boston Bulldog, will assume Cajun's role now. But he's been hiding under the bed since Sunday morning when all the crying began. The only human emotion Rebel had known in his short life was unbridled mirth—and the occasional confusion caused by memory lapses on the part of his human roommate. Such unspeakable sadness had not invaded our home in a long time.

The anguish of losing a devoted family member was too much for him, and for me. I felt like crawling under the bed with an old shoe. Instead I made Linda Barton Aultman's Whine (and Wine) Pound Cake, a culinary cure for grief. It won't remove your grief, but it certainly makes it easier to bear.

Whine (and Wine) Pound Cake

This will impart heavenly smells throughout your home while it is baking.

1 box Butter Recipe Golden Cake Mix
1 (3-ounce) package vanilla instant pudding
½ cup vegetable oil
¾ cup white wine
½ cup water
4 large eggs, at room temperature
½ cup chopped pecans
1 cup sugar
1 stick unsalted butter, melted

Stir together cake mix, pudding mix, vegetable oil, ½ cup wine, water and eggs. Spray Bundt pan with Baker's Joy. Sprinkle chopped pecans in bottom of pan. Pour in batter. Bake at 325° for 40 to 50 minutes or until toothpick comes out clean.

For glaze, dissolve sugar in melted butter, and stir in remaining ¼ cup wine. Remove cake from oven, and place on damp towel. Poke holes in bottom of cake with a toothpick. Immediately pour half of glaze on cake in pan. Allow to soak into cake for 15–20 minutes. Invert cake from pan onto a plate. Poke holes in top of cake before topping with remaining glaze, and let soak for about 30 minutes.

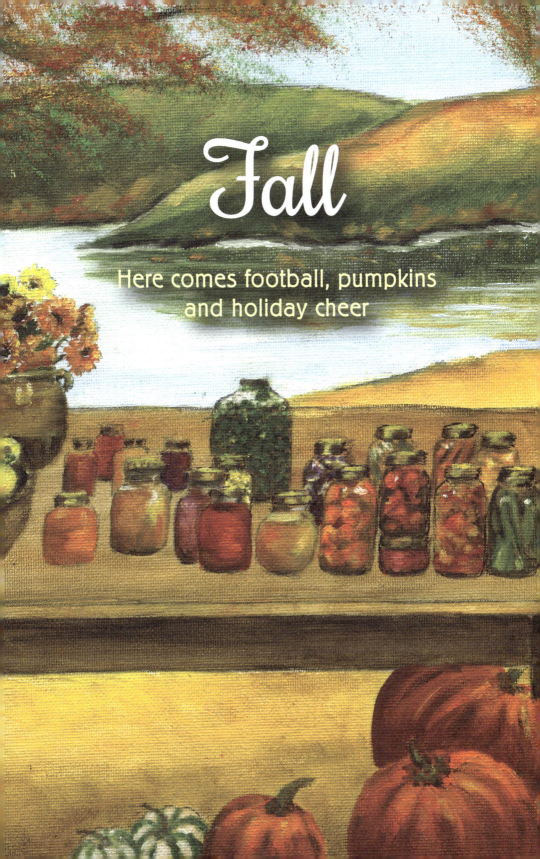

Fall

Here comes football, pumpkins
and holiday cheer

Dealing with a neurotic roommate

My roommate has been driving me crazy. I call her Motor-mouth. She babbles incessantly about everything under the sun, even when I'm trying to read or balance my bank statement.

Sometimes I go outside in a vain attempt to escape her, but she follows me right out the door, chattering on and on about the stupidest things. The worst part is I've heard it all before—maybe a hundred-thousand times.

She criticizes my clothes, nags me about my housekeeping, and questions the plans I've made for the day. She mocks me, teases me, and can be downright mean. (And my maroon tights DO NOT make me look like an ox, Miss Smarty Pants.)

I spent three hours baking a birthday cake for my son which

turned out slightly lopsided. Okay, a lot lopsided. "See? I told you this was a bad idea," she bloviated. "Why didn't you just buy a cake at the store?"

She's at her worst at bedtime. "Please hush," I beseech her. "I want to go to sleep. Why do you have to talk all the time?" Short of a concussion, sleep is the only way I can escape her constant yammering

My life's a mess because of this horrible woman who lives—not in my house—but inside my head. She's been with me all my life, but it seems as though she has become more neurotic lately and second-guesses everything I do. I've decided to initiate eviction proceedings.

This week I ran across a little book entitled *The Untethered Soul* which was written for people like me who are tired of the running dialogue emanating from their own brains. The author, Michael A. Singer, acknowledges that most of us are locked in our heads with a maniac.

"If you want it to be peaceful in there, you're going to have to fix this situation," declares Singer. "You do this by taking the entire personality that you hear talking to you . . . give it a body and put it out there in the world just like everybody else." (Mine is wearing a witch's hat and brandishing a bloody ax.)

He suggests ignoring her by mindfully engaging in something you really love and enjoy—that which makes your heart sing. For me it's digging in the garden, rearranging the furniture, or going for a walk in the woods. Eureka! Before you know it, the mean-spirited voice will be silenced and peace returns to your world.

If all this fails, I'll borrow a page from the playbook of my little bulldog, Rebel. He can spend hours staring into space or chewing on an old shoe. I'm pretty sure Rebel is smarter than I am. He's got himself a pretty sweet gig—sleeping, chasing squirrels, and getting treats for no particular reason. Of course, he also has to endure a semi-maniac for a roommate (me), but he never complains and he's always waiting at the back door jumping up and down when he hears my footsteps on the porch.

To show my gratitude to Rebel and Lucky Dawg, I often nuke up a batch of their favorite treats . . . which they call Dot Dogs.

Dot Dogs
Homemade Pet Treats

These would probably tempt the most discriminating cat as well. And frankly, they make a pretty good human treat if you're really desperate for an infusion of protein—and maybe some horse's hooves and whatever other disgusting stuff they put in hot dogs. I really don't want to know.

1 package hot dogs (you can usually find them for under $1)
One microwave
One hungry puppy

Cut up the whole package of hot dogs into half-inch rounds. Cover with a paper towel, and pop them into the microwave for 3-5 minutes.

Voila! Tasty, chewy doggy treats at a fraction of the cost of the pricier doggy treats.

Easy People Treats
Bleu Cheese Crisps

½ cup butter, softened
1 (4-ounce) container bleu cheese
½ cup chopped pecans
1 small baguette (sourdough is best if you can find it)

Mash together butter and cheese. Add pecans, and mix well. Slice baguette crosswise into ¼-inch slices. Spray with olive oil-flavored Pam, and bake at 350° for 3–5 minutes. Turn, and spread with the butter/cheese mixture and bake another five minutes until golden. My book club loves these, as they are easily made up ahead of time and popped in the oven when the first member arrives.

Parting is such sweet sorrow

They say parting is such sweet sorrow. Not so. There's nothing sweet about it. It's an anxiety-ridden, heart-palpitating, soul-wrenching experience that has turned my life upside down.

My recent separation from one of the great loves of my life has left me feeling at loose ends, and I'm having a hard time filling all the hours we once spent together. Alas, the object of my devotion had become an evil influence in my life, leading me to all kinds of unhealthy behaviors. I was letting everything else slide, including my civic duties, my hobbies, and time spent with my friends and family.

After weeks of wrestling with this difficult decision, I have pulled the plug on our relationship. I have wiped my tears and recommitted to devoting more time to exercising and spending time with other people.

Who knows, I may even do some traveling and see what's been going on in the world since I dropped everything for this toxic relationship.

Well, dawlin', this is it. It's over. So long, good-bye, adios, auf wiedersehen. I wish I could say it was nice knowin' ya, but my doctor tells me you would have killed me eventually. "Nip it in the bud," said the Doc as if he were talking about smoking or eating a pound of bacon at one sitting. He assured me I would then live to a ripe old age, just when I thought I'd already MADE it to a ripe old age.

I wasn't going to go public with the object of my adoration because I'm not proud of my inability to resist such a phony lothario. After all, I picked him up while shopping at a furniture store for Pete's sake!

His nickname is "Cat Napper," and he is a handsome red recliner which has given me many happy hours of unbelievable (albeit unproductive) enjoyment. Unfortunately, Cat has become so cozy that I have given up my exercise program and spend all my time tucked in his warm embrace, while surfing the web or reading the latest murder mystery.

My last medical check-up confirmed the bad news. It's time to get up and engage with life again. I read the other day that sitting is the new smoking, and that lounging for long periods causes our systems to shut down. My left leg has already gone to sleep.

If you have been similarly "seduced" by an inanimate object, you might want to consider an immediate breakup. The good thing is that they can't argue or talk you into taking them back.

A difficult breakup calls for comfort food. One of the first dishes that comes to mind is a delicious pineapple casserole my neighbor Brenda makes for the holidays. I'm not sure whether it's a side dish or a dessert, but it's comfort food at its best.

Breakup Pineapple Casserole

Perfect for a potluck, too.

½ cup self-rising flour
⅔ cup sugar
2 cups grated Cheddar cheese
2 (20-ounce) cans pineapple, drained, reserve juice
   (chunks or tidbits–your choice or a combination)
1 stick plus 2 tablespoons butter, divided
1 sleeve Ritz Crackers, crushed

Combine flour and sugar. Add cheese and drained pineapple, adding a little juice if mixture is too dry. Spray a 9x13-inch casserole dish with nonstick cooking spray. Place 2 tablespoons butter in baking dish, and melt in 350° oven. Pour pineapple mixture into baking dish.

In a separate bowl, microwave remaining 1 stick butter until melted, and let cool. Stir in crushed crackers until coated, and sprinkle over pineapple mixture. Bake at 350° for 30 minutes.

Savoring September

Ah, September . . . my favorite month of the entire year. It rushes in to the discordant noise of cowbells, the rhythmic beat of marching bands, and a new energy to shove out the lazy days of summer.

My thoughts turn to tailgating, spotting the first pumpkin, sleeping with the windows open, and retiring the white shoes and tank tops. Thank goodness. White shoes make your feet look like boats, and sleeveless dresses should be against the law for anyone over fifty.

I long for the smell of burning leaves, although that practice has been banned in all but very rural areas. Back in the day, before burning the leaves, we would amuse ourselves for hours jumping into the piles we had carefully raked together. If someone would come up with a fragrance called "Burning Leaves," I would buy it.

I will put up my "pumpkin tree" this week, with its little orange twinkle lights and miniature pumpkins and dare anyone to tell me I'm rushing the season. It will remain up until Thanksgiving evening, when it will change into its Christmas finery. All these things are symbols for the ephemeral notion of hearth and home so beloved by this unabashedly devout "homebody."

It will soon be time to brew up my first pot of chili, which is always a big deal when the temperatures begin to flirt with forty-five degrees. Shouldn't be long now.

All these things bring back memories of Septembers past, when my mother took me to Goldsmith's in Memphis to buy my signature pleated-wool skirt, an itchy sweater, and a new pair of saddle oxfords. Those must be the three most uncomfortable items of clothing ever produced by the fashion world. I haven't worn wool in years and probably never will again since we need something warm about one week out of the year. (I outgrew the saddle oxfords before I could break them in.)

I can still recall one crisp fall evening while I was helping Mother wash the dishes. It must have been around 1956, and Jimmy Durante was performing "September Song" in that distinctive gravelly voice. That tune must be a metaphor for life, which seems to drag along until you reach the middle ages, then speeds wildly out of control as you try to hold on to some semblance of your youth.

I am determined to slow down and savor the season and all the things that typically get trampled by my botched attempts at multi-tasking. Right now I'm craving some of Norma's No Fuss Chicken 'n Dumpling casserole. Norma is one of the best cooks in my "tribe," which is composed of anyone who graduated from West Point High School in 1965.

Norma's No-Fuss Chicken 'n Dumplings

1 stick butter
3 boneless chicken breasts
½ teaspoon dried sage
1 teaspoon salt, or to taste
1 teaspoon pepper, or to taste
2 cups milk
2 cups Bisquick
3 teaspoon Wyler's chicken granules
1 can cream of chicken soup (Norma likes Herbed Cream of
    Chicken, if you can find it)

In a stockpot, cover chicken with water and bring to a boil, then turn off heat. Cover, and allow to set for 15 minutes to finish cooking. Remove chicken from stock, reserving 2 cups stock. Shred chicken when cool.

Preheat oven to 350°. Begin layering ingredients in casserole. (Do not mix together.)
Layer 1: Melt butter in 9x13-inch baking dish
Layer 2: Spread chicken on top of butter
Layer 3: Sprinkle with sage, salt and pepper
Layer 4: Combine milk and Bisquick, and pour over all
Layer 5: Whisk together reserved 2 cups broth, granules, and
    soup. After blended, pour over Bisquick layer.
Bake for 50–60 minutes until golden brown.

Dime store to Dollar Tree:
a shopper's dream

A high point during my childhood was our weekly visit to the "Dime Store," where I would usually wind up with my nose pressed against the candy counter trying to decide which gooey confection I would sample. Back in the day, you could purchase five cents worth of nuts or candy. That was about all I could afford, since my weekly allowance was only a quarter. Fifteen cents had to go to the movie theater for Saturday's triple feature, and the offering plate at the church got the rest.

Fast forward a half century, and one of my favorite pastimes is my weekly visit to the twenty-first century version of the Dime Store. Through the magic of inflation, it is now called The Dollar Tree. It's not that I'm cheap; I just enjoy looking at things that still cost a dollar in this $19.99 world.

And I can get out of the store with a big bag of stuff without even having to break a ten.

One of the singular joys of dollar-store shopping is finding a bargain among the odd orphans of mass production. I have a complete set of water goblets I like to call "Recession glass," a take-off on the very pricey Depression glass of the last century. I could buy barely one stem of my fancy goblets for what I paid for the entire set of Recession Ware. And my friends can feel free to smash them up against the wall after a toast.

I'm especially indebted to The Dollar Tree for saving me an estimated $6,000 a year in replacement costs for my reading glasses. I buy a handful each month: one for the car, five for the home, two for my neighbor's house, and one for each of my favorite handbags. I leave them all over the place—in restaurants, at church, in the changing room of department stores. What the heck, it's the cost of doing business if you answer to the name "Deluded Diva." (By the way, my blog is www.deludeddiva.com.)

The Dollar Tree affords you the opportunity to squander your child's college fund, one dollar at a time. And you've gotta love the bizarre versions of Pepto-Bismol (Pink Bismal) and ChapStick (Chap-Ex).

Ditto for lipstick. A tube of Estee Lauder will run you about $22.50 at the cosmetic counter of a major department store, while a tube of "Este Lawyer" is a buck at The Tree. I just hope they got the lead out.

Just this week I visited The Tree to look for some horn-rimmed glasses for my Colonel Sanders Halloween costume. I came out with two bottles of Awesome cleaner (which is truly awesome), a new chartreuse cutting board for my kitchen, and a loaf of bread which would have set me back three dollars at the supermarket.

It's the thrill of the hunt and finds like these that keep me coming back for a little bargain hunting, which has become a national sport in my world.

While shopping today, I picked up the ingredients for Margaret Ann's delicious Tomato Basil Soup—which I now call my Dollar Tree soup.

Dollar Tree Tomato Basil Soup

1 can condensed tomato soup
1 can diced tomatoes with juice
⅓ cup diced onion
1 fresh garlic pod, chopped fine
Garlic salt to taste
Cracked black pepper and kosher salt, to taste
1 cup coconut milk (Margaret Ann once made this soup with heavy cream, but this is a much healthier version. She said to be careful not to use too much, or soup will be runny.)
3 tablespoons sugar
¼ cup finely chopped fresh basil

Place soup in pot. Add tomatoes and diced onion, and bring to a boil. Reduce heat immediately to low. Add garlic, garlic salt, cracked black pepper, and kosher salt. Slowly stir in the coconut milk or cream. Add sugar, and mix well. In the last five minutes before you serve, add fresh basil. The crispness of the onion and freshness of the basil make this extra special.

from human being to "human doing"

I'm dumping my "to-do" list. I mean it this time.

Now that I've retired from the nine-to-five world of reporting on fascinating and earth-shattering world events (or at least what's happening at church socials), I find that many of my working-world habits no longer serve my scaled-back lifestyle.

A friend called yesterday and invited me to dinner at a hot new restaurant. Hmmm, that would be fun, I thought. But I reflexively reached for my trusty leather-bound notebook containing a myriad of to-do lists. It was pretty full. To wit:

• Rent a carpet shampooer and get rid of the pet smells in my guest room. (I noted with alarm that this item has been on my list for the past 235 days.)

- Write my weekly newspaper column. (I'm checking that one off now.)
- Walk outdoors for one hour. (Shucks, it's raining.)
- Drink some green tea. I heard it promotes weight control, but it tastes yucky—maybe tomorrow.
- Clean out my truck. (I have systematically moved that item forward for the last 59 consecutive days.)
- And, the most dreaded of all: Floss!
- Buy cottage cheese to make Becky's Dieter's Cornbread Muffin for luncheon (see recipe on next page)

Dang it, dinner with good friends in a relaxed atmosphere wasn't on the list. Suddenly, it dawned on me that these blasted lists have ruled my life and rendered me a slave to all the "shoulda, woulda, couldas" of daily existence. I have morphed from a human being to a "human doing."

I've been an obsessive list keeper for as long as I can remember. There's one for each year, another for the month, and one for each day. Sometimes I do them by the hour. I once tried to board a plane to London without a passport, but the immigration officer wouldn't accept proof that it was on my to-do list.

I won't go into the psychology of why procrastinators like me are obsessive to-do listers, but I theorize that once we record them on paper, we somehow think they are done. I wondered what would happen if I boldly approached a new day without a list . . . if I just lived each magical moment without attacking it with the vengeance of a vigilante.

I read somewhere that you should do your list each day, and then cross off everything that is unimportant. Heck, if I did that, I would have a blank page!

So yesterday I operated free-style and did only what the spirit moved me to do. I was like a skydiver in free fall without a parachute, a sailor without a compass. My headstone should read "Got it all done, died anyway." That little thought always helps me put things in perspective.

My "to-do" list today includes a little advance preparation for a luncheon for some dieting friends. You'd think by now we'd have given up on being thin. But the old adage about never being too rich or thin never dies a proper death in my crowd. Thanks to Becky Wilkes for giving me a recipe that I love, low calorie or not (two muffins have only one Weight Watchers point!).

Becky's Dieter's Cornbread Muffin

These cornbread muffins border on the miraculous and almost seem like a science project since they only contain two tablespoons of cornmeal – yes, you read that right.

⅓ cup cottage cheese, small curd is best
2 tablespoons self-rising cornmeal
1 egg, beaten

Mix and bake at 400° for 15 minutes until golden. I like to use mini muffin pans. Go ahead and double or triple to serve 4–6.

Good news for lollygaggers

Well, strike me pretty and call me Sophia Loren! A new book, destined to become a best seller, claims that procrastination may be a good thing. That sound you hear is me clicking my heels as I dump my tax forms in the waste can where I keep all the important stuff. It's my personal filing system, and I typically deal with it when the can gets full.

Being a world class slacker and habitual tarrier myself, I decided to order the book. Hopefully I'll get around to it next week if it doesn't rain.

This is great news for all of us slackers, lollygaggers, dawdlers, piddlers, and stallers, who can proudly come out of the closet and procrastinate without guilt. Procrastination can make you a better person, according to John Perry, author of *The Art of Procrastination*. You can safely put off everything that can wait until tomorrow and engage in whatever it is that floats your boat at the moment. Music to my ears, for sure.

The key idea is that procrastination does not mean doing absolutely nothing. Procrastinators do all kinds of useful things. We sharpen our pencils and make diagrams of how we will reorganize our closet when we get around to it. We make endless lists of what we need to do and pick out the easy tasks to do first.

But be aware that if all the procrastinator had left to do was to sharpen some pencils, no force on earth could get him to do it. So why do some people (me included) behave this way? Because there's always something we would rather do, even if it's just a catnap.

The book reveals that the chronic procrastinator can be motivated to do difficult, timely, and important tasks . . . as long as these tasks are a way of NOT doing something more important.

Did you follow that? You will finally make an appointment for your annual physical when faced with a deadline to get your taxes done. You'll finally do your taxes when faced with a need to make a dental appointment etc., etc., etc.

Mild procrastination, apparently, can produce a latent energy that can lead you in a new and more effective direction. So I submit that procrastination fosters creativity.

This week I decided to test the theory. I was committed to cleaning up my back courtyard, which has taken on a dump-like quality, the result of collecting too many things I found on the side of the road or picked up at garage sales. There's a plethora of ravaged stuff—like that three-legged iron chair. But it was so cute, and I figured I could get someone to make a fourth leg for it (eight years have passed, and I haven't found anyone yet).

So, I did what I could. I put it on the street for someone else to pick up and keep for another eight years. I figure this is how antiques survive into the next century, and I feel I have performed a service for future generations. In a nutshell, I have become a "structured procrastinator," a person who gets a lot done by not doing other things.

The best part about procrastination is that you are never bored, because you have all kinds of things that you *could* be doing to avoid things you *should* be doing. Besides, you'd be really hacked off if you got your taxes done and let the dentist into your mouth with his drill, only to have a wayward asteroid crash onto your corner of the world.

If you're looking for a good lollygagging recipe, here's one to try. It's great for one of those days when the grandchildren are coming over and all you have in the house is a box of moon pies.

Moon over MSU

1 Moon Pie (any kind will do but chocolate is my fave)
1 scoop ice cream
Sundae topping (whatever floats your boat–fudge is mine)

Place Moon Pie on a plate and microwave for 12–15 seconds. Watch in awe as it rises to form a crater in the center. Place a scoop of ice cream in the crater and douse with your favorite sundae topping. We call this Moon over MSU because Mississippi State University is located in my town.

The great spice cabinet cleanout

Erma Bombeck said, "Once you get a spice in your home, you have it forever. Women never throw out spices." Right on, Erma, I'm proof positive.

It came to me about ten hours ago as I attempted to prepare the obligatory mashed sweet potatoes for Thanksgiving. I added the nutmeg as usual, and I might as well have added pencil shavings. The nutmeg had no flavor whatsoever. I turned it upside down to check the expiration date and almost fainted. It expired about the time I turned forty, which was during the Reagan administration.

I began checking the date on the other four dozen tins of spices stacked three layers high and four rows deep above my stove top. Some were so old they didn't even have expiration dates. The only spices still viable were the garlic powder and something called Slap Ya Mama seasoning, which my son gave me last Christmas. Think he was trying to tell me something?

There was outdated apple pie seasoning, and I don't ever recall making an apple pie. Isn't that sad? There were half a dozen cans of poultry seasoning (all expired), which I must purchase each year before making the Thanksgiving dressing.

No wonder my would-be culinary masterpieces often fall flat. All my spices and herbs are stone-cold dead. The frugal side of me did not want to toss the spices, but the practical side convinced me it was necessary.

> PRACTICAL REASON #1: No one should eat something that is thirty years old.
> PRACTICAL REASON #2: Spices should have a scent.
> PRACTICAL REASON #3: Green herbs should not be beige.
> PRACTICAL REASON #4: Expired spices don't need to be replaced. I obviously wasn't using them anyway.

All the expired tins and jars immediately got a proper burial . . . in the trash can. They weren't even suitable for the compost pile. Even my Tabasco had turned brown.

The most puzzling thing is that I had no idea what some of the spices should be used for, if ever. There was mace, which I probably bought for protection against some unsuspecting burglar. There was something called anise, which I don't recall ever using. Ditto for cardamom, which is a mystery.

My can of turmeric was purchased when I heard Julia Child say it was good for improving your memory. She died in 2004, and my memory has grown progressively worse since then.

I read somewhere that a tin of something exotic in your cabinet hints at a well-traveled individual. More likely it reveals a crazy person trying hard to be a modern day Julia Child. I suspected as much the minute I tried to cook pasta in the coffee maker. Clearly, I'm missing the gene to be a great cook. No, make that an average cook.

So what's reasonable regarding the storage of spices? McCormick shares these guidelines for how long spices can be expected to last.

- Seasoning blends: 1-2 years
- Herbs: 1-3 years
- Ground spices: 2-3 years
- Whole spices (such as cinnamon sticks and peppercorns): 3-4 years
- Extracts: 4 years (except for pure vanilla, which lasts indefinitely)

McCormick also warns never to store the spices in a warm place. The cabinet above my cook top is the warmest place in the house. Well, no wonder . . .

Once all the spices were carried to the street in a garbage bag, I headed to the grocery store to begin rebuilding my seasoning supply. All I really need is salt, pepper, garlic powder, and lemon pepper. Oh, and I will need some more poultry seasoning for the dressing. I think I'll just go ahead and throw it away after measuring out a teaspoon for the dressing.

My friend Ginger Jones has a wonderful recipe that will help in the crusade to clean out the spice cabinet. She served it to our book club and everyone had a fit over it.

Crescent Lasagna

1 pound ground beef
1 medium-sized onion, chopped
1 clove garlic, minced
1 tablespoon chopped parsley flakes
½ teaspoon each: oregano, salt, and pepper
1 can tomato paste

For meat filling, brown ground beef in a large saucepan, and drain. Add remaining ingredients. Simmer uncovered for 5 minutes.

1 cup cottage cheese (small curd works best)
¼ cup grated Parmesan cheese
1 egg, beaten
2 cans crescent dinner rolls
1 cup shredded Mozzarella cheese
Sesame seeds to taste

Mix cottage cheese, Parmesan, and egg to make cheese filling. Unroll crescent rolls; place on ungreased cookie sheet. Overlap edges slightly to form 13x15-inch rectangle. Press edges to seal.

Spread meat filling lengthwise down center of dough to within 1 inch of each 13-inch end. Top with cheese filling. Place mozzarella over cheese filling. Fold 13-inch ends of dough over filling by 1 inch. Pull long sides of dough rectangle over filling, being careful to overlap edges only one quarter inch. Pinch overlapped edges to seal. Brush with a little milk, and sprinkle with sesame seeds. Bake at 375° for 20–25 minutes or until deep golden brown.

The dangerous world of static cling

After being out later than usual on a recent Saturday night, I slept in Sunday morning, promising myself I would go to church Sunday evening.

About eleven a.m. I began to rally and discovered I was out of eggs.

I pulled my favorite hoodie out of the clothes dryer and rushed over to the Piggly Wiggly. As long as I was there, I wandered through the store picking up a few items I needed for my family Thanksgiving dinner, which was less than two weeks away.

Old friends who had attended early church were trickling into the store, and I felt a twinge of guilt about my unchurchly appearance.

We chatted about football and mundane things like the weather. I knew I was getting a lot of attention, and I was thinking it was my heretofore unnoticed effervescent personality. Everyone seemed to be staring at me. Oh, boy, I must look good today, I thought.

As I waited in the checkout line, a friend two aisles over whispered as quietly as she could while pointing to her upper back: "Emily, you have a bra hanging out of your hood."

At first it didn't compute. I looked at her blankly until her message reached my brain. Oh, my God! (Not a good time to call on Him; He had just played a good prank to teach me a lesson about skipping church.) I reached back and pulled the wayward bra out of my hood and stuffed it into my pocket. I wanted to throw it on the floor and stomp on it, declaring, "It's not mine!"

I glanced around frantically to see if anyone else had noticed.

EVERYONE had noticed! The other shoppers were practically in tears, trying to conceal their glee. I turned a shade of maroon that would have pleased the head coach of Mississippi State University. If it had been a nice frilly bra, it might have been okay, but this was one of those old serviceable models I should have discarded before 9/11. But it was so darn comfy. I certainly never expected the world to see it in the middle of the supermarket, on a Sunday morning no less!

Even the bag boy couldn't control his guffaws. An elderly man behind me patted my shoulder and said, "Honey, I wanted to tell you, but these days young people sometimes wear their underwear on the outside."

"WELL, NOT ME," I wanted to scream.

I have never been more humiliated, but at the same time it was pretty funny. I laughed out loud all the way home. I walked over to tell my neighbor Brenda about my latest gaffe (she's keeping a list). Between tears, she said, "You know what that looks like, don't you? Looks like you had a pretty wild time last night."

Oh, gee. I never thought of that. But I learned a valuable lesson. Never cut church without a good reason and always, always check your hoodies for hidden articles of clothing. If it had been my Godzilla panties, I would have died on the spot.

I also learned that God has a wicked sense of humor. I can hear a big "GOTCHA!" in the sky. I went right home and began tossing together Mary Jo's Butterfinger Pie, which involves beating up candy bars with a rolling pin. What else would help me forget this awful experience? Oh, and I'll be burning the bra.

This sounds like the perfect time to pick up ingredients for Margaret Ann's Cranberry Wine Salad. It's a delightfully different way to present the obligatory cranberries at Thanksgiving.

Cranberry Wine Salad

1 (3-ounce) package raspberry Jell-O
2 cups boiling water
1 cup port wine
1 large can crushed pineapple, do not drain
1 can whole cranberry sauce
½ cup toasted chopped pecans
1 cup finely chopped celery

Dissolve Jell-O in boiling water. Cool slightly, then add port wine. Let cool until almost thickened. Stir in remaining ingredients. Place in greased mold, and chill until firm (about 6 hours). Yields about 10 servings, and is great for holidays . . . especially when the in-laws are coming.

A picture perfect
Thanksgiving (almost)

I've been doing Thanksgiving for my family for twenty years—ever since my grandmother died. Nobody could do it like she did, but I've been trying to recreate her magic ever since.

Each year I come close. Yet I always manage to burn something or forget to cook something. Or, like one year, I baked my requisite Spinach Madeline in a non-ovenproof dish and the bottom fell out when I took it out of the oven. I ruined a new pair of suede shoes which will forever be tinted green and smell like spinach.

But this year, it all came together. I began a week ahead, cooking the cornbread for the dressing, making and freezing casseroles, polishing the silver, and building a holiday centerpiece. I piled my dining room table with dozens of small pumpkins I found on sale at Walgreens (three for a dollar). Now I know why they were on sale. They smelled like dirty socks. But my table looked stunning.

This was shaping up to be the year I could finally make my Mam-ma proud. Then, my new friend Elizabeth Gwin told me how she's been preparing her cranberries for ninety-plus years (yes, no typo, she's 105 and still going strong). She spreads them on a cookie sheet and sprinkles them with sugar and roasts them until they "pop."

How fun! So at nine p.m. on Thanksgiving Eve I ran over to the grocery store to get some fresh cranberries. As I wandered through the store, a nice lady stopped me and told me she enjoyed my newspaper column and felt she could relate to my foibles. I was so distracted to learn that someone actually READS my column that I followed her through the store. We chatted, and I completely forgot what I had come for. I got home with a six pack of Diet Coke, a bunch of green onions . . . and no cranberries.

But the good news: I was ninety percent finished with my holiday preparations—and not a single mishap. This was going to be MY YEAR. I surveyed my table one more time on Thanksgiving morning. Perfect, except I'd forgotten the good salt and pepper shakers. I got out the silver ones, which never see the light of day except on holidays. They were so corroded they looked like pewter. I polished them up and dried them off.

Hours later, I refilled the shakers with fresh salt and pepper and set them on the table. I decided to leave the tops off a little longer to make sure no moisture remained. One hour and counting: the company began arriving. No problem, casseroles were resting at 200 degrees, ice was in the goblets, and I was cool as a cucumber.

Oops! I forgot to light the candles. The first lesson my mother taught me at the age of five is that it is *gauche* to have new, unlit candles in your home. You must at least light the candles and blow them out (to appear, I suppose, that you didn't buy them just for the occasion, which of course I did).

I lit my votives and blew them out, and in the process spewed salt and pepper throughout the dining room. Everyone began sneezing, and a cloud of pepper was raining down on my perfect Thanksgiving table. Okay, so not everything was perfect, but as glitches go, this was pretty mild. We still talk about what we now call "The Sneezing Thanksgiving."

If you want to try something different for your holiday table, here are my Nawlins Filet Mignyams. They were a nice change from the usual sweet potato casserole with marshmallows on top. The recipe came from my New Orleans period, where folks call sweet potatoes "yams." I don't think that's technically correct since they are actually two different animals, but who cares? I love anything wrapped in bacon.

Nawlins Filet Mignyams

4 medium yams or 8 small ones
8–12 slices bacon

Boil yams in skins until tender. Cool and peel. Leave small potatoes whole, cut medium potatoes in halves or thirds. Wrap each piece in bacon, securing ends with toothpicks. Bake on rack in shallow pan in moderately hot oven at 400 ° for 15-20 minutes, or until bacon is done and crisp. I think next time I will cook the bacon a little bit before wrapping the yams to cut down on the fat. Serves 8.

Aunt Emma's Insanely Easy Two-Ingredient Holiday Candy

Here's an insanely easy two-ingredient holiday candy that everyone will think you spent hours fussing over! You can make these blindfolded with one arm tied behind your back.

½ package chocolate bark (you may use either dark chocolate or white chocolate flavor; she usually does one of each)

2 cups peanuts or roasted pecans, your choice

Place chocolate bark in a microwave-safe dish and nuke on HIGH for approximately 2 minutes, until well melted. Add nuts, and stir until all are coated in chocolate. Drop by teaspoon onto waxed paper and let set until hard. They freeze well and are great for tailgating (and for making people think you spent a whole day making candy).

"Leon, Leon" the angels did say

I collect funny stories. Not jokes, mind you. I really don't like jokes all that much.

The few times I've tried to repeat a joke, I botched the punch line. Everyone rolls their eyes and snickers politely. But a real-life funny story stays with me forever.

My favorite one was told to me by Kate, the one whose *crotch* pot turkey breast (a.k.a. her "sick dish") is on the next page—her housekeeper always called the slow cooker a "crotch pot." Anyway, Kate loves to tell the story about the day she put out her Christmas decorations, including some children's wooden blocks to spell NOEL. She placed them lovingly on her mantle and went out to do some Christmas shopping.

Imagine her surprise a couple of hours later when she

returned home to find the blocks rearranged to spell LEON. Apparently the housekeeper missed the significance of NOEL and put them back from left to right. Who knows? Maybe she was dyslexic. I think of that story every time I hear "The First Noel."

That story almost tops what Mama M (my second mother) did during all the holiday madness. She accidentally swallowed her hearing aid battery instead of her monthly dose of Fosamax. Then there was my friend Robert, who "maced" himself when he borrowed a car to run an errand. He glanced on the seat and saw what he thought was a can of breath spray. You can imagine the rest of the story.

These and other true stories are filed up front and center in my cerebellum so I can pull them up when depressed or caught in a long line somewhere. Yes, I'm laughing like a hyena, and my fellow shoppers figure my elevator doesn't go all the way to the top. I guess they're correct. It probably doesn't get to the third floor.

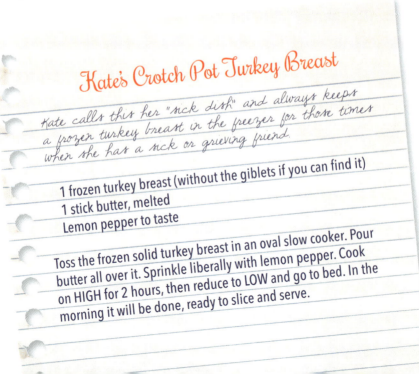

Kate's Crotch Pot Turkey Breast

Kate calls this her "sick dish" and always keeps a frozen turkey breast in the freezer for those times when she has a sick or grieving friend.

1 frozen turkey breast (without the giblets if you can find it)
1 stick butter, melted
Lemon pepper to taste

Toss the frozen solid turkey breast in an oval slow cooker. Pour butter all over it. Sprinkle liberally with lemon pepper. Cook on HIGH for 2 hours, then reduce to LOW and go to bed. In the morning it will be done, ready to slice and serve.

The
Fifth Season

Baby Boomers Busting Loose

If you're under 50 you might want to skip this section.
It was created for Baby Boomers (those born 1946–1964)
and their older friends and family members.
We find that this is the best season of all.

Just so you'll know, there aren't but a couple of recipes in this section because my fellow boomers and I rarely cook anymore. We usually order pizza.

The feisty side of fifty

Along with the arrival of balmy spring weather, four of my best friends and I celebrate our birthdays together each year. We have been friends for five decades, and suddenly we have landed on the feisty side of fifty.

I've noticed that my baby boomer bosom buddies and I are growing increasingly adventurous. No painting by numbers or Friday Night Bingo for this crowd. We seem to have lost our inhibitions and matured into a bodacious bunch wandering into an unexpected second childhood. So far, it's shaping up to be better than the first!

No longer confined by careers or focused on raising children, we are discovering that a vast frontier looms ahead. It is beckoning us to hone new interests and make new friends. Suddenly, the nest is empty, and we are free to do all the things we were too busy (or too timid) to do even a decade ago.

Not being the most adventurous person of my generation, I'm experimenting with semi-wild things like drinking from the garden hose, running with scissors, and taking candy from strangers. You wake up one morning and realize you don't give a hoot what others think, a discovery which can sometimes entice you to cross the line on decorum.

On a whim, four of us recently climbed up the giant silver pony which was erected in front of a "gentlemen's club" over near Mayhew Junction. We didn't go into the establishment, mind you. We just had our pictures made while we were riding high in the sky and looking ridiculous.

Why did we do it? Because someone said we couldn't. Becoming a dinosaur has its privileges. Passing trucks honked at us, and the sheriff passed by and waved. If we'd been fifteen, he probably would have hauled us in.

Not too long ago we had a sleepover at my house—first one since we were seventeen. At two a.m. we all piled into one car and went to Walmart to buy matching pajamas. The checkout lady asked if we were the Sweet Potato Queens. We told her we were their first cousins, the Turnip Green Goddesses. She asked for our autographs.

Who could imagine that aging would be so liberating? Dare I suggest it is more fun to be a senior citizen than a teenager? We are baby boomers busting loose, yes ma'am! We can have the car anytime we want it, and so what if we put a dent in the bumper? We can throw a raincoat over our pajamas at midnight and ride over to the Sonic for a hot fudge sundae without asking permission.

We are no longer burdened by the overwhelming urge to please others at our own expense. We can share our deepest secrets freely, secure in the knowledge no one will remember them after about twenty minutes. My biggest fear is that one day soon I will forget which comes first . . . long pants or underwear! By then, though, I won't care.

If you're old enough to have seen *I Love Lucy* or The Beatles the first time around, you are probably on the feisty side of fifty, too. If you don't want to go to a party, just don't go. You can tell them it slipped your mind and they will believe you.

Through it all, we try to remain faithful to our ideals and strive to give back more than we take. Life after fifty is better than I ever imagined. As Cliff Eastwood said in one of his rough and tumble movies, "Every day on this side of the dirt is a good day."

By the way, we do not consider ourselves over the hill; we're just now celebrating our peak. All aboard, boomers. It's going to be a wild ride.

The aging of conversation

Last weekend, six of my childhood friends journeyed to the Mississippi Gulf Coast to visit a seventh classmate. As usual, we engaged in a bit of laughter therapy and spent most of our time wandering down memory lane (which grows longer and more crowded with each passing year).

The weather was picture perfect and there was a whole exciting world out there to enjoy. There were shopping centers at every intersection, pristine beaches beckoning us to take off our shoes, and flashy casinos just waiting to feed us watered-down drinks and take our money.

Tempting as all this was, we opted to sit around the breakfast room table, eat pimento cheese sandwiches, and talk about the way we were before we got the way we are.

My little group met in a sandbox a lifetime ago under the watchful eyes of our doting mothers. We shared dolls, clothes, boyfriends, and gossip; we walked hand-in-hand through that perilous passage from childhood to adulthood. Then we lost touch as husbands, careers, and children got in the way.

Suddenly, about ten years ago, we began to reestablish our friendship. We'd get together a couple of times a year and found it enormously refreshing and cathartic. Once, we met on a houseboat in Austin, Texas, and another time on the ski slopes of Jackson Hole, Wyoming. We even spent two nights with a classmate who lives in the Chancellor's home at the University of Alabama. No, she wasn't the maid; she married the Chancellor, who is also an old chum. Olivia and Mack Portera treated us like royalty and we danced to Chubby Checker, made a royal mess, and figure we won't be invited back until we are too old to kick our heels up quite so high.

Like riding a bike, it's easy to slip back into the silliness of our youth, and do things we would never think of doing back home where folks think we are mature, responsible citizens. And because our brain cells have declined with each passing decade, it requires that each of us dig down deep to dredge up our personal memories. We come away with a pretty good composite of our history together, and the laughter grows more hysterical with each passing year.

Somewhere around nine p.m. on Friday evening, we had exhausted our teen years, our early adulthood, and the Middle Ages. Finally we got around to the current state of affairs, which we thought was pretty dismal . . . until we discovered that aging is a team sport, and our team just got its second wind.

One moment we were talking about who we dated in high school, and then the conversation took an ominous twist into the land of blood pressure medication, orthopedic shoes, and wrinkle cream. We pondered whether Medicare would still be around when we get to the ripe old age of sixty-five. I wish I could say we have a long way to go, but I'd be lying.

It suddenly dawned on us that our topics of conversation have aged right along with our bodies.

In retrospect, it seems that one day we were cutting out paper dolls, and the next we were receiving our AARP cards. What happened in between is a blur—until those special times when we are together and a delightful past catches up with us.

One of our favorite activities is remembering our mothers, who are all gone now except for one. We still cook up some of their favorite recipes, which traveled through our community like wildfire during the 50s and 60s then faded into oblivion. We've brought many of them back again and I'm always surprised how many people have never heard of dishes like "Copper Pennies."

The Copper Pennies recipe dates to the 60s. I love them because you can make it up two weeks in advance. If you're not up to all that scraping and boiling the carrots, it's perfectly fine to use canned carrots (approximately four cans, drained).

Copper Pennies

5 cups sliced carrots
1 medium sweet onion, sliced
1 green bell pepper
(10-ounce) can cream of tomato soup
½ cup salad oil
1 cup sugar
¾ cup white vinegar
1 teaspoon prepared mustard
1 teaspoon Worcestershire sauce
1 teaspoon salt
1 teaspoon black pepper

Boil carrots until just tender. Drain, and cool. Cut onion and bell pepper into round slices and mix with cooled carrots. Mix remaining ingredients, and pour over vegetables. Cover, and marinate for at least 12 hours. Drain before serving. I use the reserved juice for salad dressing on those busy days between Christmas and New Year's. Serves 12.

Remembering the olden days

As the years fly by, remembering where I put my car keys has become a challenge, but the memories of growing up in Small Town, Mississippi, are as crisp and clear as a summer morning.

Today, as temperatures hover around ninety, my thoughts take me back to my childhood . . . when television was not a 24/7 presence and the term "personal computer" was still two decades away. Telephones were all landlines—what else could they possibly be? Some of my friends were lucky enough to have what we called "party lines," where several families shared a line and you could eavesdrop on your neighbor's conversations. That was loads of fun.

You've probably figured out by now that I've been infected

with a new disease called acute nostalgia. As far as I know, there is no treatment or relief from the condition—except to spend as much time as possible with others afflicted by the syndrome. That pretty much includes anyone who grew up in the 50s and 60s and remembers clothes blowing in the wind on the clothesline out back and playing hide and seek at dusk. You could be decapitated by those same clotheslines as you darted across the neighbor's backyard to get back to home base.

In those days everybody loved *I Love Lucy* and *Father Knows Best*. We would make ourselves a Coke float, sit on the davenport, and hum along with cool cats singing "Doo Wah Diddy Diddy." So-called art in those days featured framed prints of dogs playing poker.

I loved watching Dinah Shore sing "See the USA in Your Chevrolet" when the average cost of the family car was a mere $2,749, and brace yourself . . . gasoline was only twenty-four cents a gallon! A guy once told me that a car with fins guaranteed him a date with the cutest girl in the class.

But there was more to the 50s than sock hops and milkshakes delivered to your car window by a girl wearing skates. For one thing, there was no swearing on TV. In fact there was no swearing in life. I was once grounded for a week for saying "double darn," and that's no lie. (I only say *no lie* because it's come to my attention that some people think I make this stuff up.) I was grounded for two weeks for sneaking into a limited showing of "Splendor in the Grass." Oh, the shame!

Those were the days when the whole family sat down for dinner every night and occupied the very same pew in church each Sunday. Heaven help the stranger who dared sit in your place. Incidentally, it was true what the rest of the world thought about us hicks in the south—we didn't wear shoes from May to September except for Sundays, and there was no pain like being caught in a patch of stickers on a hot summer afternoon. You could miss supper (dinner was served at noon) waiting for someone to come rescue you.

My nose remained sunburned from May to September and I fully expect to come down with skin cancer any day now. We lounged around in the sun wearing a homemade suntan lotion concocted from baby oil and iodine. Why in the world would you want something called sunscreen? That was counter-intuitive to our 50s way of thinking. The whole point was to sport a nice, rosy painful glow, oblivious to the dangers.

We had just been introduced to the Frisbee and the hula hoop. My best friends and closest neighbors Phil, Heard, Martha, Lota and Larry would have "fop fights" every Satur-day morning. In case you haven't had the pleasure, a fop fight is when you take all the leftover copies of the *Daily Times Leader* from Phil's paper route, wet them down, and pummel each other until you're black and blue. Boy, was that fun or what? Martha is gone now, and the rest of us have joined the ranks of retiree. How did it happen so fast?

But the memories come flooding back when I hear the buzzing of a bee, which is a rarity these days. Where have all the bees gone? And the frogs . . . they were everywhere in the 50s and the boys used to taunt us with them. The worst feeling in the world was when Phil put one down my tank top. (Inci-dentally, the wearing of a tank top by me will occur about the time evolution eliminates the human little toe.)

So what do you remember about your childhood? What sparks your return to the child who still lurks inside? I won-der if your memories are similar to mine and half as wonder-ful. I feel like the luckiest woman in the world to have been allowed to grow up in Small Town USA, where women never cussed in public, the men only spit in the wind, and the children could play for days without an internet connection.

Lost in Paradise

I'm having a serious problem with losing things . . . er, make that *misplacing* things. My home has become the proverbial black hole, gobbling up anything that has any value.

I'm writing my memoirs (entitled *The Land of the Lost*) as I search without luck for my 2012 tax return and my Day Timer—which means I don't know where I'm supposed to be and when. Typically, this leads to a frantic search that ends with all my furnishings turned upside down.

I lost one half of my favorite earrings, so I wear the other one along with a pretty close facsimile to the lost earbob. (Did I just say earbob? No one ever says that these days.) Oh, great, now I'm losing my once-stellar command of the English language.

I lost one of my shoulder pads and cringe to think what people must have thought when it slipped out. Now I'm all lopsided with one big shoulder and one small one. (I'm well aware shoulder pads went out with the mullet, but they're great for anyone suffering from the dreaded pear shape. They are necessary to help equalize the top with the bottom.)

I'm also having problems remembering the name of certain common household items. I was trying to describe that thing that sticks to your ceiling and turns in circles to keep the air moving and couldn't pull it up. Finally someone suggested "ceiling fan" and looked at me as if I might be coming down with scarlet fever. Hey, maybe that's what's causing my memory lapses, and not something more sinister. Sometimes I'm not sure if I found a rope or lost my horse!

My favorite red handbag has gone missing along with my safe deposit box key and I wonder if they ran off together. I've been paying the annual rental fee on that lock box for twelve years and have no idea what's in there. It caught up with me last week when the bank was bought out, and I was instructed to come remove the contents of the box. Now I'm really busted—wonder if I can pick that lock with a bobby pin. (There I go again. Have you heard anyone refer to a bobby pin in the last twenty years?)

I've left pairs of reading glasses all over five states and in the District of Columbia. I've lost my debit card twice, once in the drive-through box at CVS and once in the pocket of my jeans which got washed on "hot."

Life has become like one long game of Charades when it comes to remembering "Ole What's His Name." You know the one—he's married to that redheaded girl with a Swedish accent who walked like this (you demonstrate her walk and suddenly someone remembers Ole What's His Name's name). You could remember every detail about the fella, but in my world no one has names any longer. I say, "Hey Girl," or "Hey Fella," when I run into someone I'm supposed to know, and pray I got the gender correct.

It's possible that this is just a natural byproduct of our busy lives, but it seems to be cropping up with greater regularity with each passing year. I keep thinking how nice it would be to lose a few pounds instead of my glasses.

Never offer a female a senior discount

I got a big dose of déjà vu yesterday while standing in a long grocery line. I had three items: a bottle of Clairol, some wrinkle cream, and the economy size of ginkgo biloba—nary a thing to eat. That's what happens when you grow older . . . food no longer matters as long as you can afford every new anti-aging product that comes down the pike.

But that's beside the point I need to make. An acquaintance (much younger) was in front of me in line and we had been one-upping each other about all the fascinating things we're currently involved in. She is training for the Nashville marathon and asked how Marie and I trained for it—blah, blah, blah.

I bragged that I'm into whitewater rafting these days

because running is too hard on the knees. (Editor's Note: We truly did complete the Music City Half Marathon, but I didn't tell her we walked the last nine miles and crossed the finish line on all fours.)

So, she finally gets to the front of the line and plunks down her Generation X probiotic yogurt and vitamin water. The gum-popping, hot pink-coiffed clerk rang her up and asked if she wanted the senior discount. I watched that poor girl (my acquaintance) deflate like a punctured tire. In a pitiful state of exasperation, she angrily ran her bank card through the machine but couldn't remember her pin number.

I felt so sorry for her I wanted to take her in my arms and say, "There, there. The clerk didn't mean it. She's probably not wearing her contacts." (Secretly I wished I could see that clerk when she gets payback around the age of forty-five.)

The truth is, the exact same thing happened to me fifteen years ago when I was still way too young to partake of the dreaded senior discounts. The difference was, I had a truckload of groceries when the well-meaning clerk asked if I wanted to take the senior discount. She might as well have said, "You look like an ugly old dried-up prune of a bag lady, so let me make your day and give you a nickel off your loot."

I looked at her in horror then slammed my purse shut and stomped out into the parking lot to look for my car, which took me twenty minutes because I was seeing red. See what happens when someone offers you a senior discount? You mysteriously age thirty years on the spot. I left that entire cart of groceries on the conveyer belt and vowed never to return to that grocery store in this lifetime. (Interestingly, it went out of business a few months later.) I also made an appointment for hair color and renewed my prescription for Retin-A.

I eventually got over the incident and these days, I'm tickled to death to get a few bucks off, though I'd rather *ask* for the discount. I don't want anyone volunteering it. That will instantly clue you in that you're a) needing your roots touched up; b) it's time to book a weekend for a "Lifestyle Lift"; or, c) begin wearing turtlenecks and gloves and never take off your sunglasses.

The moral of this story, for all you well-meaning retailers, is NEVER ask a woman if she wants the senior discount. If she qualifies, she knows it and will ask. A ten-percent discount just isn't worth the pain of admitting you've reached the dark side of the hill.

The disappearing woman: Is sixty the new sixty?

Somewhere during the last decade, I seem to have been erased and replaced by an imposter who has taken on the drabness of the foggy morning sky.

I walked by a busy construction site this morning expecting a few suggestive hoots. All I heard were flies buzzing around looking for a tasty morsel. No whistles, no catcalls. I might as well have been a stray cat creeping by.

You've heard the hype about how sixty is the new forty, or fifty is the new thirty. It's more likely that sixty is the new sixty—and I'm overdue for my 60,000 mile tune-up.

When did I become a bad copy of my former self? Maybe I should dress in flamboyant reds and yellows and dump the sweats. Do people (especially women) become invisible around age sixty?

I'm a good girl. I pay my bills on time. I follow the rules and never park in the handicapped spaces. Yet I feel I'm off my game. So I did what any practical woman would do under the circumstances . . . she goes shopping.

I waltzed into the department store and instantly became dizzy. Swirling around the display were orange polka dots and cotton candy pinks. The large graphic prints assaulted me and set my teeth on edge.

Determined to buy a dress, I pulled a nice pink frock off the rack and did a double take. Had I wandered into the children's department? Beside it was a cute little paisley number, but little was the operative word. The company must have run out of fabric because the skirt was less than twelve inches long. Maybe it was a blouse, I don't know.

I noticed a beautiful voile piece but you could see slap through the fabric. My church would excommunicate me for indecent exposure. I got the attention of the young clerk—no small task when you are the invisible woman. I asked where I could find more classic styles. Like the kind Grace Kelly would wear.

She gave me a blank stare and mumbled, "Who's Grace Kelly? Is she a model or something?" I left the store without trying on a single garment.

Embracing old age isn't bad if you can appreciate your accrued wisdom and feel comfortable in skin that has mysteriously become two sizes too big.

I guess dignity has become overrated. According to a recent magazine article, "dressing old" can make you feel and behave older. Most people try to dress appropriately for their age, so clothing in effect becomes a lightning rod for ingrained attitudes about age. I guess it's better to be a mutton dressed as a lamb than a mutton dressed as mutton.

If you were a Girl Scout of the 1950s, you harbor a tender spot in your soul for the beloved S'More. You remember it, don't you . . . the campfire staple which sandwiched graham crackers with burned marshmallows and half a Hershey Bar. My forty-something friend Brian Hawkins has developed his own version of the S'More, which is pure genius. I make them up for those times I don't want to feel sixty-something.

Brian's S'More Clusters

2 (12-ounce) bags milk chocolate chips
½–¾ (13-ounce) box Golden Grahams cereal
½ bag miniature marshmallows

Place chocolate chips in a microwave-safe bowl and microwave until melted, stirring once or twice. Stir in cereal, and mix thoroughly. Fold in marshmallows, and drop by tablespoonfuls onto ungreased cookie sheet. Refrigerate until hard (about 15–20 minutes) if you can stand it.

Mirror Mirror—
Give me a break!

Now that I've passed to the dark side of forty, I've begun to buy into the idea of remedial skin care to help undo the damage I've done while sunbathing, laughing, smiling, crying, and breathing—all my favorite activities.

While wandering through Bed, Bath & Beyond last week, I happened upon an innocuous-looking display featuring "essentials for the boudoir." Right in the dead center was a lighted makeup mirror with a sign bragging that it would magnify an object fifteen times.

I casually glanced into the mirror to check my lipstick. What peered back at me was so grotesque I jumped back and shrieked loudly enough that the store manager started dialing 911.

My son William was with me. As he helped me up off the floor he whispered to me gently, "Mother, why do you do this to yourself? It multiplies every minor imperfection by fifteen."

I didn't care. I bought it anyway.

That mirror has revealed a pockmark leftover from kindergarten when I was the first to contract chicken pox. Mother was so proud. I also discovered that my lips don't match. The right side stops short of where the left side continues, which leaves me with a permanent smirk. If you see me smirking, don't take it personally.

Those Middle Eastern women have a good idea. Know where I can purchase a burqa?

I went through the hat box, which serves a burial ground for all my castoff "Bottles of Hope," none of which worked. They carry names like Renova, Reclaim, and Regenerist. It all made me want to regurgitate. I poured them all into one jar and slathered them on my face.

This morning I rushed to the 15X magnifying mirror and saw the same face I saw yesterday.

I'm beginning to appreciate the brilliant idea behind declining eyesight which sets in about the time we turn forty. I'm proposing that we ban eyeglasses at our next class reunion. That way, the lines will blur and we will all look fabulous.

Aging disgracefully

L ife is like a roll of toilet paper. The closer to the end you get, the faster it goes.

The year 2012 was a milestone year for the Class of '65 because we were about to reach age sixty-five—so it would be easy to remember. (Not that we'd ever tell the truth about our age.) How did we get there so fast? Seems like yesterday we were playing baseball in my front yard and today we woke up feeling like a ball that had been batted around.

Here it was already September and my "bucket list" had no check marks. A feeling of urgency set in, and I figured it was time to get out of my comfort zone (my easy chair) and get living.

My old gang from high school tries to do something we've never done before at least once or twice a year. Since we've been taking line dancing lessons, it sounded like a good fit to head up to the hinterlands of Arkansas to attend a Dulcimer festival and do some folk dancing and hiking. That should be good for a few laughs.

It's amusing how our bucket list has changed radically since AARP got our addresses and began bombarding us with material intended for old people. Previously we bought into the lofty dreams of jumping out of an airplane (with a parachute attached, hopefully), riding the whitewater rapids in British Columbia, or scaling the mountains of Nepal. Suddenly these items seem hopelessly unrealistic—unless we want to go deep into debt and end up eating cat food stroganoff.

So we rationalized that there isn't much difference between Arkansas and Nepal. We also did some serious editing on our bucket list. Instead of renting a villa in Italy, we'll be staying in a cabin loaned to us by a friend in the foothills of the Ozarks. I hope it has indoor plumbing.

We'll be doing a little fishing and foraging for mushrooms and wild berries and who knows . . . if we're lucky we may have a close encounter with Bigfoot, post it on the internet, and get interviewed by all the media outlets.

Instead of getting cosmetic surgery to correct our laugh lines, we'll create a diversion by putting our clothes on backwards. That way no one will notice the wrinkles because they'll be so confused by our troubling attire. I got that idea last night when I wore two different shoes to my book club and no one even noticed that my grey roots were showing. But, hey, both my shoes were black. Doesn't that count for something?

Instead of driving to Florida for some beach combing, we'll drive through the wrong end of the car wash. Oh, wait, we've already done that. Instead, I'll just turn on my left turn signal and leave it on all day. That always messes with people's minds. Instead of discussing a great work of literature, we'll talk ad nauseam about the outrageous price of gasoline and the weather. Have you noticed how old people do that?

I think all these bucket list items are doable before the end of the year. In the meantime, we'll be revealing all our dirty little secrets with each other this week in the mountains, knowing full well no one will ever remember them when we get home.

Born to be wild

As the months and years fly by, the reality of aging has suddenly hit me like a cold north wind. So I button up my jacket and hope the jacket I'm wearing is my own.

The time has come to let go of some of the outdated rules of conduct that have ruled my life for too long.

I've never run around in the house with scissors, or worn white shoes before Memorial Day. And I would never, ever wash my darks with my whites.

We get only one life, and I've been living mine on low beam. Maybe it's time to walk on the wild side, let my imagination run wild and toss convention to the winds.

To test my new modus operandi, here's what I did this week to break the rules and walk on the wild side:

• I rode a bike without a helmet. (Okay, so what if the bike was glued to the floor, inside the gym.)

- I walked the treadmill at the same gym without holding on to the rails. I tried chewing gum at the same time, but maybe I'm not ready for that just yet.

- I went to a movie all alone. I've never done that in my entire life. Unfortunately I couldn't stay because the picture was so badly out of focus. (Couldn't be my eyes. No way.)

- I went to McDonald's and bought a cheeseburger and fries without guilt. Of course, in true Senior fashion, I had dinner at four p.m. and ordered from the $1 menu. Now that was exciting!

- I cooked a gourmet dinner for friends wearing a strapless gown. Unfortunately, I spoiled the effect by wearing sweats underneath.

- I wore my iPod to the Piggly Wiggly even though the batteries have been dead for two years. It irked me that the checkout clerk thought I was wearing a hearing aid.

Undaunted, I drove home, put on a pair of baggy jeans, a sideways baseball cap, and danced along to a hip-hop video on MTV. For the first time in his life, my bulldog, Rebel, broke into a wide, toothy grin!

Where did my world go?

I saw a segment on CNN recently about the top twenty-five innovations that have changed our lives profoundly during the last quarter century. Things like the cell phone, the laptop computer, the ATM, lithium batteries, e-mail, and DNA fingerprinting.

Personally, my list would have been a bit different. I would have cited Lean Cuisines, long-wearing lipstick, Spanks, and pop-top cans as more significant in my world.

I detest the cellphone; I've never learned how to use my laptop without plugging it in the wall; unless the lithium battery is in my hairdryer, who cares?

But the CNN story ricocheted off the left corner of my brain and lodged in the right side, conjuring up a wave of nostalgia that left me breathless. I pulled up things that I took for granted during my formative years. Now they represent a sort of mental archaeology I hadn't dug up until today.

I recall the times even before the rotary dial phone, when you just picked up the receiver and a friendly voice said "Number, please." I would say "Three-twenty-seven, please," to connect with my best friend. We would chat ad nauseam about what to wear to school the next day or who got caught chewing gum in class. After thirty minutes or so, the friendly voice would break in and say "Emily, you need to get off the phone. Mrs. Hudson's gall bladder is acting up again."

Daddy was one of four town doctors and, well, it was time to get off the phone.

Then I thought about the clotheslines that bisected the backyards of every lawn in my neighborhood. They were treacherous, particularly on warm summer evenings when we would play hide and seek. You could be decapitated darting across the lawn to avoid being "it."

I remembered Halloween trick-or-treating when the best treats didn't come in carefully-measured packages—but were delivered warm from the oven. Word got around fast which house had the best stuff. We tripped all over each other getting over to Mrs. Vance's, who gave out popcorn balls. We carried bars of soap but weren't sure what to do with them.

I thought about the dishwasher, which reminds me of my aproned mother humming "Begin the Beguine" while gazing from the kitchen window. What was a Beguine anyway, I wondered, but never asked.

I thought about how everyone envied me when I got my first Hi-Fi and two Johnny Mathis records. They had a big hole in the middle that had to be plugged up with a plastic thingy to fit on the turntable.

I remembered our first Color TV. It was an old black and

white set on which a piece of acetate had been taped on the screen. It was color-coded with pink at the top, red in the middle, and green on the bottom.

I thought about that $300 set of World Book Encyclopedias my parents gave me for my eleventh birthday. I thumbed through them for hours sitting in the back porch swing while Daddy mowed the yard with something that looked´like an egg beater.

Using the velocity of my brand new saddle oxfords, I pumped and pumped and dreamed of a future when someone might walk on the moon and my Hi-Fi would stop skipping when Frankie Avalon hit a high note.

My mind couldn't fathom what would happen in the next half century, and I'm getting nervous thinking about what technological surprises are ahead down the road.

"Many men go fishing all of their lives
without knowing that it is not fish they are after."

—*Henry David Thoreau*